THE ANATOMY OF
THE SWIPE

THE ANATOMY OF THE SWIPE

MAKING MONEY MOVE

AHMED SIDDIQUI

NEW DEGREE PRESS

Illustrations by Nicholas Straight

THE ANATOMY OF THE SWIPE
Making money move

ISBN   978-1-64137-447-7 *Paperback*
         978-1-64137-448-4 *Kindle Ebook*
         978-1-64137-449-1 *Ebook*

CONTENTS

———

***

HOW TO READ
THIS BOOK

———

Whether you are an entrepreneur looking to impact billions of people globally, or an engineer who's just plain curious about the payments space, this book aims to break down how card-based payments work. This is a nonfiction book that describes very real payments situations through stories, pictures, and comics. The book can be read sequentially or skipped around, depending on your level of knowledge or interest.

BOOK SEGMENTS

The book is broken down into five main segments:

ANATOMY OF THE SWIPE

This segment describes what is actually happening when you swipe your card at your favorite restaurant.

Read this if you want a high-level understanding of what happens during a swipe and how the money moves during settlement.

PAYMENTS ECOSYSTEM

This segment will break down all of the parties involved to enable card-based transactions.

Read this if you are new to payments and want a good overall understanding of the parties involved and what their roles are.

DIGGING DEEPER

Once we have a good understanding of what happens during a card swipe and the parties involved in making it work, we'll take a step deeper to understand the actual mechanics and economics of the transaction.

Read this if you already have a good understanding of the payments ecosystem and want more details on a specific topic like card types, Interchange calculations, know your customer (KYC), and bank-to-bank money movement.

PAYMENTS IN ACTION

This segment gives examples of how payments are applied to create innovative solutions to real problems. More content like this will be available as supplements on the *Anatomy of the Swipe* website:

www.anatomyoftheswipe.com

Read this segment by itself to give you some ideas on how you can apply card-based payments to your business.

GLOSSARY
All key terms defined within the chapter are also available in the glossary. It will also reference the chapter(s) where these terms were mentioned for context.

Read this if you want to skip around to learn about a specific topic.

CHAPTER STRUCTURE
Each chapter will be structured to aid in comprehension, and most chapters flow as follows:

- **Recap:** Brief recap of what happened in the previous chapter
- **Key Question:** The central question we are trying to answer throughout the chapter
- **Key Terms:** Payments-related terms are defined
- **Story Time:** Payment concepts explained in terms of a fictitious story
- **Founder Stories:** Some chapters will contain stories of founders and how they got into payments
- **Key Takeaways:** Summary list of the main things discussed in the chapter
- **Up Next:** Quick sneak peek into the next chapter

* * *

INTRODUCTION

———

What would happen if you had a real financial emergency?

A surprise expense, whether it's an unexpected medical bill or an emergency house repair, can ruin anyone's day. For most of us, these bills require a creative dance of moving around some money to get us through the month. But for a large population of Americans, these expenses can be disastrous. Twenty-eight percent of US adults have no emergency savings, according to Bankrate's latest Financial Security Index.[1] Even if they do have emergency savings, 57 percent of Americans don't have enough cash to cover a $500 unexpected expense.

Khaleel, a manager at a discount retailer, was part of that 28 percent of Americans. And he was in trouble.

"It was six o'clock in the morning and my car broke down. I had $25 to my name and about $5 in my bank account. I get paid every two weeks."

———

1   "Bankrate survey: Just 4 in 10 Americans have savings they'd rely on in an emergency," Jill Cornfield, Bankrate, accessed on January 26, 2020.

For people like Khaleel, historically his options have been scarce and often very punitive. Usually limited to predatory payday lenders or perhaps borrowing from family. Oftentimes, small bumps in our lives can cause someone to lose everything—their homes, their kids, and their livelihood. When more than half of Americans live on the razor's edge, it can be an incredibly scary world. But technology, an ever-opening financial system, and enterprising innovators have begun to offer new approaches for people like Khaleel.

In a matter of seconds, Khaleel was able to receive $150 to his Visa debit card from Branch, a mobile technology providing earned wage access and other financial services. Moments later, he was able to make a swipe and pay the mechanic with his Visa debit card to get his car fixed. With another card purchase, he was able to get into an Uber to get himself to work.

We rely on credit and debit cards almost daily but rarely think about what needs to happen for a swipe to turn into a successful transaction. This book will take an in-depth look into how card-based payments work, from the Merchants who want to accept payments to the banks that issue millions of cards a year to consumers wanting to transact by using a piece of plastic in their wallet.

While the world primarily runs on cash, card-based payments enable the world to run faster. In 2017, 5.5 trillion dollars was transacted annually with debit and credit cards in the US alone, according to Nilsen research.[2] In Khaleel's case, if he didn't use the card-based technology offered by Branch, he would have been late to work or even fired. Cash just wasn't an option for him.

WHO IS THIS BOOK FOR?

Whether you are an entrepreneur looking to impact billions of people globally or an engineer who's just plain curious about the payments space, this book aims to breakdown how payments work. This is a nonfiction book that describes very real payments situations through stories, pictures, and comics. Every major tech company at some point will need to interact with the payments ecosystem, and I hope you can use this book as your guide to understanding and implementing payments systems at your company. We'll be taking a deep look at what happens in the three seconds when someone swipes their card at the card terminal of their favorite restaurant. We'll also be looking at new technologies like Push-to-Card, Peer-to-Peer payment, and new ways of authorizing transactions in the cloud, based on things like geofences and Artificial Intelligence. Furthermore, we'll take a look at the revenue models for companies utilizing payments.

ALL MODERN TECH COMPANIES ARE PAYMENTS COMPANIES

Card-based payments enable us to purchase goods from anywhere in the world and get it delivered right to our doorstep.

---

2   "Payment Cards in Circulation Worldwide - Projected," Nilson Research, October 2019, Issue 1162, accessed on January 26, 2020.

Payments technology companies such as Stripe, Finix, and Marqeta are getting massive valuations from the investment community as they continue to power these modern commerce experiences. In fact, over $40 billion in Venture Capital money was invested in payments and fintech companies in 2018 alone.[3]

Companies such as Airbnb, Uber, Lyft, DoorDash, and Instacart have armies of people working on payments to make commerce as friction-free as possible for their customers. On deeper inspection, these companies actually ARE Payments Companies.

The act of swiping a card to purchase something seems pretty simple, and to many, it is pretty mundane. However, if you can understand the details of what is happening within those three seconds, a world of opportunity opens up. The reality is that the payments space is complex and hard, but people like Jack Dorsey, Chief Executive Officer (CEO) of Square, Jason Gardner, CEO of Marqeta, Atif Siddiqi, CEO of Branch, and Zach Perret, CEO of Plaid took the time to really understand these nuances and are unlocking massive opportunities.

SNOW, SAND, AND SWIPES: HOW I LEARNED ABOUT PAYMENTS

Why should you listen to me? Well, let me tell you the story of how I got entangled in the world of card-based payments.

---

3   "Fintech: The Fourth Platform - Part One," Matthew Harris, Forbes, accessed on January 26, 2020.

In 2014, at my San Francisco apartment near AT&T Park, I was on the phone with a trucking company, arranging to ship my car to Minnesota. My daughter, Misha, was about to turn one-year-old, and my wife, Mona, and I had decided we should move to Minnesota to be closer to my parents so my daughter could grow up with her cousins. I had already given notice to my previous employer and gave my thirty-day notice to my landlord.

Suddenly, the red alert badge showed up on my Facebook app. I opened up my Facebook app and there it was, a message from my old high school friend, Dave Matter. After reconnecting with him on Facebook a year earlier, I found out he'd moved to the San Francisco Bay Area as well and started working at a company called Marqeta. Not many people I knew from Coon Rapids High School, or Minnesota for that matter, moved out to the Bay Area. I hadn't spoken with Dave since 1998 on the day of graduation; unfortunately, I wasn't the best person to keep tabs on high school friends.

He asked, "So when are we getting this coffee?"

I replied, "Tomorrow? I'm pretty free these days."

He agreed but later asked to move the meeting to the following week.

I responded, "I don't have too much time, as I'm moving to Minnesota." So, he moved his other appointments around so we could meet up at Farley's in Emeryville for coffee, right around the corner from Marqeta's original offices.

As I was driving over the Bay Bridge to meet up with my old friend, I was thinking, *Geez, we won't have enough time to really catch up in one hour. High School was so long ago, and we have got way too much to catch up on!*

When I got to Farley's, one of the first things Dave said was, "How can I convince you not to move back to Minnesota?"

I froze a bit. All our bags were packed, movers were coming in a week, my wife even gave her resignation, and my parents were eagerly awaiting spending more time with their one-year-old granddaughter.

What initially started as a high school reunion, quickly became a job interview. Dave proceeded to tell me more about what he'd been up to at Marqeta. At first shot, I didn't really understand it. I just responded, "So you do something like Stripe?" Stripe was the darling of the payments world back in 2014. It allowed developers to easily accept card payments on their websites. I didn't know much about the payments ecosystem at the time, so Stripe really was my only reference point. Instead of explaining what Marqeta does, he just demonstrated it.

Dave has a "professor-like" quality about him. He's exceptionally good at describing how things work and can be incredibly convincing. Dave pulled out a Blue debit card with a "+M" logo on it and began to explain. "Okay, so I just loaded up $50 that I can use JUST at Farley's. When I loaded $50 on this card, it actually gave me a value of $55, which is a Merchant bonus. When I go to buy this coffee, you will see that the value goes down and I'll get a text message of the balance."

He swiped his debit card at the register. Immediately a text message popped up on his iPhone that said, *You spent $8 at Farley's, your Farley's balance is $47.* The professor hadn't convinced me yet. I replied, "So what? My Chase credit card has the same type of alerts."

He then opened an app on his iPhone to show that not only did he now have a $47 balance at Farley's but also a $98 balance at Piedmont Grocery. "You see, I'm only spending money from my Farley's Purse, and not touching the balance I have at Piedmont Grocery."

"Ohhh, okay, so you can keep multiple balances on one card!" I exclaimed. Now, he had me intrigued but still skeptical. I've actually heard this idea probably ten times before at various Startup Weekend events I ran through the years, but I've never seen it actually implemented in a very elegant way. But again, what he was showing me still felt like a nice feature, I couldn't think of this becoming a real business. Plus, was it really something so interesting that I would cancel my move to Minnesota?

Dave went on to explain that a number of tech companies are using this technology as a platform to build their own cards.

Now, all of a sudden, a feature became a platform. Other companies could use the platform that Dave built to build their own features. At this point, the professor had me enchanted. He then asked, "Do you know anything about malls in Dubai?"

Immediately, I visualized vast malls with ski hills and ice-skating rinks in the middle of a desert. I nodded.

Dave continued, "Well, we are about to sign a deal with them to do a mall card where we can offer similar types of purse functions for different stores and restaurants in the mall."

I told him, "Oh, that's funny you mentioned that. It's always been on my bucket list to work in a Muslim country..."

Dave leaned in and asked, "Are you sure you still want to move to Minnesota?"

So, after my meetup with Dave, I took my wife, Mona, out to dinner at Chaat Cafe in San Francisco and asked her, "What would you rather have, the snow or the sand?"

Initially, she was confused by the question. She was really looking forward to moving to Minnesota so she could get some help raising our daughter, and Minnesota is still closer to Connecticut, where her parents are.

Obviously, this was a huge shock to her, but after a bit of explaining, she agreed that this could be an opportunity of a lifetime to live in the Middle East while working for a Bay Area Tech Startup. She would need to put her own plans on hold. As a pharmacist, she wasn't sure if she could even practice in Dubai and had concerns about getting back into the field when we moved back.

The good news was that my daughter was still pretty young, and we didn't need to worry about school yet. In many ways, I don't think I could have gotten into payments had it not been for my wife's openness to the adventure of living abroad and coming along for the startup journey.

That night, I called Dave and told him, "We'll take the sand."

I received an offer from Dave the following day as Director, Product Management at Marqeta. I canceled my movers and found a temporary apartment in San Francisco close to the Bay Bridge entrance.

Now, with all the logistics taken care of and a job offer in hand, reality sank in. I knew nothing about payments...

Dave convinced the entire team at Marqeta that I could head up the office in Dubai. I couldn't let my friend down. I took in a deep breath and started my search on Google. As I kept searching and researching, I kept getting more and more confused. There just wasn't a good definitive guide to understanding this stuff. The next day, I went on a walk with Dave and sheepishly admitted, "Dave, I'm in over my head already. How can I learn more about payments? I don't want to let you down."

Dave assured me that the feeling was normal. In fact, the vast majority of the early employees at Marqeta did not come with a payments background. A lot of people actually came from Imagine Games Network (IGN), a video game media and entertainment company. He took me into a conference room and drew out the ecosystem on the whiteboard:

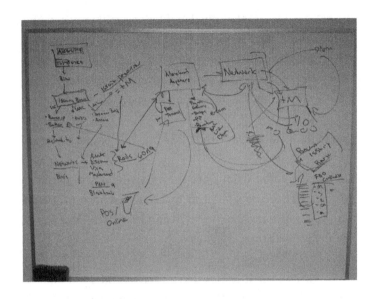

Yeah, even after this drawing, I was totally lost...

After this, he handed me this book from Glenbrook Partners titled *Payment Systems in the US*, which to this day serves as the textbook for anyone getting into payments. The challenge I had with the book stemmed from me being a visual learner. I just couldn't get my head around how everything worked.

I still couldn't figure out what the difference was between Marqeta, Stripe, Square, and even for that matter, PayPal. Until finally, Tony Ford, Marqeta's Chief Technology Officer (CTO) explained it as this: Stripe is a Gateway and gives you application program interfaces (APIs) and tools that enable you to *Take* payments—that is, if you have a website that sells coffee beans from all over the world, you could use Stripe to accept payments on your website. Marqeta is an Issuer Processor and has tools and APIs that allow you to *Make* payments—that is, you can use Marqeta's APIs to create the credit or debit card that would allow you to buy those special coffee beans from Yemen.

It took me a bit of time to understand what this actually meant, but after drawing it out probably at least one hundred times, I fully understood it. The hope is that I can explain the vast world of payments by sharing these drawings with you throughout the course of this book.

Fundamentally, payments can be made very personal because we all interact with payments on a daily basis. Being originally from Minnesota, I'd use familiar references to Minnesota companies like Target, Dairy Queen, and Best Buy—to which my co-workers would always make fun of me for but at least they remembered these stories.

I spent my first thirty days at the company trying to absorb as much as I could from my peers. In the early days, the company was very small with only thirty-five people, and most of us didn't have any previous experience in payments. In a way, we were all learning about payments together.

Around the thirty-day mark, I was in Las Vegas for Startup Weekend's Organizer Summit and I got a call from Jason Gardner, Marqeta's CEO. "Ahmed, we are getting on an Emirates flight on Sunday evening to Dubai to close this deal, where are you?" Knowing Dubai has a formal business culture and all I had packed were some Startup Weekend t-shirts and shorts, I changed my flight back to San Francisco so I could quickly run to my apartment and repack. Then I hurried back to the airport to get on the sixteen-hour

Emirates flight to Dubai with Jason Gardner, Eric Bachman, Marqeta's Chief Operations Officer (COO), and Errol Pinto, also on the product team at Marqeta.

Upon our arrival, we ended up signing the deal with the mall operator in Dubai. The project was going to kick off in two weeks and would take place over the course of at least two years. As it didn't make sense to put things in storage, Mona and I scrambled to sell off and give away most of our personal possessions, but we still ended up with around ten suitcases. We then tried to spend as much time as possible with our friends in the Bay Area before we embarked on a brand-new Airbus A380 double-decker airplane to Dubai before beginning my journey into Payments.

In Dubai, my days were spent working with the mall operator, designing a loyalty program and card program. Working with the card manufacturer, Oberthur, to figure out how we could print cards on the fly at the guest services desks in the mall. Working through certification requirements with Mastercard. Finally, negotiating contracts with Emirates NBD Bank to ensure that they would sponsor the program. At night, I'd be on calls with Errol Pinto on the product team back in the US to make sure that development for all of our APIs and apps were on track. Steve McNabb and Jatin Salla from the engineering team would help me understand how all the integrations would work technically so I could relay this information back to the mall operator's engineering team.

Most of our existing products were running on the Discover network, so the relationship with Mastercard was still new. What I also learned is that finding people at Mastercard (and later even at Visa) who knew how Issuing worked was really difficult. This is because both companies are so large that everyone there knows only their part of the business. Most things are documented; however, for us in the early days, the documentation didn't make sense. Because we couldn't find someone who could talk us through it, we made a lot of mistakes. After all, we were relatively nobodys in the space. Those mistakes turned out to be invaluable and really helped us get a good understanding of how things actually worked... Something that even the most comprehensive guides from Visa or Mastercard wouldn't tell us.

We completed our integration with Mastercard and Oberthur in Dubai, completed User Acceptance Testing with the mall operator, and were ready to launch. But after the 2015 New Year's celebration, we were told that the project was put "on hold" indefinitely and that we would receive payment "Inshallah" (God willing).

We made a huge investment in setting up an office in Dubai. Countless flights to and from San Francisco from the leadership team. The entire company worked around the clock to bring this program live. For an early-stage startup, this was a huge blow and we didn't have the cash flow to maintain an office in Dubai, and most importantly, didn't have time to wait for "Inshallah."

I had failed my friend. He entrusted me to head up the office in Dubai, and I couldn't even get this program live. Mona and I had gotten rid of our rent-controlled lease in San Francisco. We would have to start all over again in the Bay Area. That is, if I still had a job...

I disappointedly packed up all ten suitcases with Mona. We had a caravan of taxis going to the airport with our luggage and flew back to San Francisco. I'd spent so much time and energy establishing Marqeta in Dubai and building a really amazing product for the mall operator in Dubai. But in the end, I was grateful to have struggled through all of this because it helped me gain a great understanding of how payments worked.

While my experience in Dubai didn't yield any business for Marqeta, the relationship we built with Mastercard and the tooling we built in Dubai was key to really finding our product-market fit. Shortly after this experience, we were able to sign amazing tech companies like Affirm, Kabbage, DoorDash, Instacart, and Square as customers. In many ways, losing the business in Dubai was a blessing in disguise. In 2017, Visa made a strategic investment into Marqeta, and in 2019, Marqeta became valued at over $1.9 billion.

CHAPTER 1

PAYMENTS ECOSYSTEM OVERVIEW

WHAT'S NEEDED TO ENABLE A CARD-BASED SWIPE?

The payments ecosystem can be complicated; however, it can be broken down into easily digestible pieces. When we talk about payments, we will primarily be referring to card-based payments. Before we get into our example, understanding a few key concepts will be helpful.

Fundamentally, four major things must exist for a card payment to work. Note: these same things apply for both credit and debit cards:

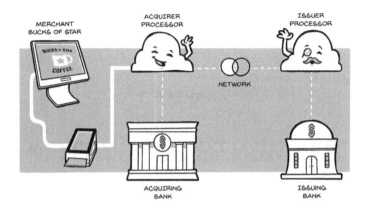

1. First, you need a card that is issued by a bank:
   a. Sometimes it could be a physical piece of plastic with a magnetic stripe at the top and/or a chip.
   b. Sometimes it could be a virtual card that is just the card number shown in an app, which can be used for online transactions.
   c. Sometimes the card could be tokenized, meaning that it is a card stored in the phone's wallet like Apple Pay or GPay and then used to "Tap and Pay."

Key Term: Issuer
An Issuer or Issuing Bank's function is to underwrite the user by giving them a bank account, a debit card, and potentially access to credit facilities and a credit card. Examples include Citibank, Wells Fargo, US Bank, and Chase.

Key Term: Issuer Processor
The Issuer needs a technology provider that can connect with the payment networks. Usually, the Issuer Processor will have a piece of hardware

in their data centers and a fast network connection directly to the payment networks to approve or decline a transaction. Sometimes, the Issuer may have built this technology in-house or may rely on a third-party Issuer Processor to handle this. Examples include Marqeta, Tsys, Galileo, i2c.

2. Second, the Merchant, if they have a physical location, needs a machine that can read the card that is provided by an Acquirer:

   a. Sometimes referred to as a card reader.
   b. Sometimes referred to as a card terminal.
   c. Sometimes referred to as a payment terminal.
   d. Sometimes referred to as a Point of Sale (POS).
   e. For online Merchants, this is referred to as a payment gateway. This isn't a physical machine in this instance but rather it is handled via software.

   Key Term: Merchant Acquirer
   The Merchant Acquirer goes out and acquires Merchants and provides them the tools and facilities to accept and process card-based payments. Examples include Citibank, Wells Fargo, US Bank, and Chase.

   Key Term: Acquirer Processor
   The Merchant Acquirer needs a technology provider that can connect with the Payment Networks. Usually, the Acquirer Processor will have a piece of hardware in their data centers and a fast network connection directly to the Payment

Networks to request approval of a transaction. Sometimes, the Merchant Acquirer may have built this technology in-house or may rely on a third-party Acquirer Processor to handle this. Examples include Chase Paymentech, Tabapay, and Fiserv.

3. Thirdly, the linkage between the card and the card reader is the Payment Network, such as Mastercard or Visa.

   Key Term: Payment Network
   Sometimes referred to as a "Card Scheme" or just as a "Network." Examples of Payment Networks include Visa, Mastercard, American Express, and Discover. These Payment Networks provide the rails for card-based transactions to occur. They sit in between Acquirers and Issuers and pass messages back and forth to make the transaction happen. The Payment Networks also set the communications rules and standards that the Acquirers and Issuers need to adhere to.

4. Lastly, a secure Internet connection for all of these messages to transmit back and forth. Now, this is done via Ethernet or even a Wi-Fi connection but in the past was done over the phone lines via dial-up connections.

To better understand the anatomy of the swipe, let's look at an example:

Emmet is a young professional living in San Francisco working in the tech scene. He starts his morning off by taking a walk down the Embarcadero where he goes into San Francisco's Ferry Building to buy a coffee at Bucks of Star Coffee. In his wallet, he has a Mastercard debit card from Moneybin Bank. He arrives at Bucks of Star Coffee in the morning. The Ferry Building is bustling with people getting on and off ferries with people scurrying off to work or getting on another train to continue their journey.

Something is magical about Bucks of Star Coffee's mocha; the perfect temperature, the smoothness of the chocolate, and coffee that is slow dripped to make the perfect start to any day. Emmet buys a mocha for $4.75 and swipes his Moneybin Bank Mastercard at Bucks of Star Coffee's payment terminal. When that swipe occurs, he sees the word "Authorizing" on the payment terminal. This typically stays in this state for three seconds or less, but within those three seconds, a lot is happening.

A message goes from the payment terminal to its Acquirer Processor with the amount of the transaction, location of the transaction, Merchant type, and the card number. The Acquirer Processor then determines that this is a Mastercard and routes it to the Mastercard Network.

Mastercard then sees this transaction and based on the card's number, it looks for the first six digits of the card, also referred to as the card's Bank Identification Number (BIN). Mastercard determines that this BIN belongs to Moneybin Bank.

Mastercard sends a message to Moneybin Bank with the card number, amount of the transaction, location of the transaction, and Merchant type.

Moneybin Bank's Issuer Processor then looks at this data and makes a decision on whether this transaction should be approved. The key things it will ask based off of the information it has received from Mastercard are:

- Does Emmet bank with Moneybin Bank?
- Is Emmet's card active?
- Does Emmet have enough money in his account to cover the cost of this transaction?
- Can Emmet's card be used at this Merchant?
- Does this transaction raise any sort of fraud flags based on location, prior activity, or type of Merchant?

If all of these questions get answered favorably, then Moneybin Bank's Issuer Processor will send back a message to Mastercard that the transaction is approved. It will place a hold of $4.75 on Emmet's account and the transaction will appear as "Pending" on Emmet's statement.

Mastercard will then relay this decision from the Issuer to the Acquirer.

The Acquirer Processor will then send a message to the payment terminal to approve the transaction. The terminal then flashes the word "Approved," and typically it prompts Emmet to sign for the order, or a paper receipt is printed where he can sign.

This transaction flow will serve as the basis for a lot of our discussion on the anatomy of a swipe.

SO HOW DID EMMET GET THIS CARD?

Emmet first needed to get a debit card for all of this to work. Issuers like Moneybin Bank distribute cards and underwrite the transaction on behalf of Payment Networks. The Payment

Networks rely on Merchant Acquirers to get as many card terminals into the hands of as many Merchants as possible.

IDENTIFYING EMMET: KNOW YOUR CUSTOMER (KYC)

In this case, since Emmet was using his debit card, it is most likely that Emmet walked into the physical location of a Moneybin Bank (the Issuer) to open up a checking account. When opening up a checking account, Emmet was asked a series of questions that helped identify him. This is commonly referred to as the KYC process, or "Know Your Customer" process. In the US, the key means of performing KYC is by getting the following pieces of information from the user:

- Name
- Social security number
- Date of birth
- Physical address
- Phone number
- Potentially some other form of identification like a driver's license, a passport, or government-issued ID

This is done primarily to prevent bad actors from entering the financial system. It checks to make sure that Emmet isn't funding terrorist activity or hasn't participated in money-laundering activities.

Once Emmet passes the KYC process, Emmet is then asked to deposit some funds into the checking account so he can start using his debit card or write checks.

CARD TRANSACTIONS ARE AUTHORIZED BY AN ISSUER PROCESSOR ON BEHALF OF THE BANK OR CARD PROGRAM MANAGER

Moneybin Bank uses an Issuer Processor to process transactions. In the case of Moneybin Bank, they have multiple Issuer Processors, but we'll discuss at length some more modern Issuer Processors like Marqeta to understand how transactions are actually authorized and where opportunities lie.

TRANSACTIONS ARE INITIATED BY AN ACQUIRER PROCESSOR VIA A GATEWAY OR PAYMENTS FACILITATOR

Bucks of Star Coffee uses Square for its terminal. Square is not an Acquirer Processor but rather a Payments Facilitator. We'll talk at length about Square and its capabilities as a Payments Facilitator and how it interacts with Chase Paymentech, its Acquirer Processor.

We'll then talk about what it means to be an Acquirer Processor and opportunities in the space by looking at a modern Acquirer Processor, Tabapay. We'll also look at some of the new technologies Acquirer Processors like Tabapay are offering to its customers.

THE CARD NETWORKS ACT AS THE "RAILS" TO MAKE ALL OF THIS WORK

Finally, we'll do an in-depth look at Mastercard and where it sees card payments going. We'll also talk about opportunities the Network is opening up for Issuers, Acquirers, and its consumers.

KEY TAKEAWAYS

- A number of parties are involved in enabling Emmet to buy his mocha with his debit card including:
  - Card Networks—Visa, Mastercard, Discover, and American Express.
  - Merchant Acquirers—The companies that provide payment terminals for Merchants like Bucks of Star Coffee so they can accept card-based payments.
  - Issuers—The companies (usually banks) that distribute cards and underwrite people like Emmet.
- There actually is a lot happening in the three seconds it takes for Emmet to swipe his card to the time the transaction is approved.

UP NEXT...

A deeper look into what happens at the time of the swipe or the Authorization.

PART 1

ANATOMY OF THE SWIPE

CHAPTER 2

ANATOMY OF THE SWIPE PART 1: AUTHORIZATION

———

Every day, 338 million transactions take place where products or services are purchased with a card, according to the Federal Reserve Payments Study 2018.[4] This could be a debit card or a credit card used by:

- Swiping it—the card's magnetic stripe is slid across the card reader.
- Dipping it—the card's chip is inserted into the card reader.
- Tapping it—the card, mobile phone, or smartwatch is tapped on a contactless terminal.
- Entering it—typing it into a web browser to buy something online.

---

4   "The Federal Reserve Payments Study - 2018 Annual Supplement," Federal Reserve, accessed on January 26, 2020.

BUT WHAT IS ACTUALLY HAPPENING WHEN THIS SWIPE, DIP, OR TAP OCCURS?

How is money taken out of your account and into the hands of the coffee shop owner?

> *Key Term: Authorization*
> *Authorization happens at the moment of the swipe, dip, or tap at the payment terminal. This action typically places a hold of funds on the cardholder's account if the cardholder has enough money in their account, or it may decline the transaction if the cardholder doesn't have enough money in their account or if other restrictions are on this type of spend.*

Let's closely examine what happened when Emmet dipped his card for $4.75 at Bucks of Star Coffee:

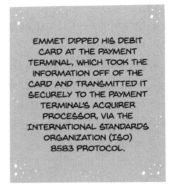

EMMET DIPPED HIS DEBIT CARD AT THE PAYMENT TERMINAL, WHICH TOOK THE INFORMATION OFF OF THE CARD AND TRANSMITTED IT SECURELY TO THE PAYMENT TERMINAL'S ACQUIRER PROCESSOR, VIA THE INTERNATIONAL STANDARDS ORGANIZATION (ISO) 8583 PROTOCOL.

THE ACQUIRER PROCESSOR THEN TOOK THAT DATA AND MADE A DETERMINATION THAT IT IS A MASTERCARD TRANSACTION AND SENT THE DETAILS OVER TO THE CARD NETWORK, MASTERCARD.

MASTERCARD THEN RECEIVED THAT MESSAGE FROM THE ACQUIRER PROCESSOR, AND DETERMINED THAT THIS CARD WAS ISSUED BY MONEYBIN BANK. MASTERCARD DID THIS BY LOOKING AT THE FIRST SIX DIGITS ON THE CARD, REFERRED TO AS THE BIN.

MASTERCARD THEN SENT THE MESSAGE OVER TO MONEYBIN BANK'S ISSUER PROCESSOR.

MONEYBIN BANK'S ISSUER PROCESSOR THEN FOUND THAT THIS ACCOUNT BELONGS TO EMMET, AND PERFORMED THE FOLLOWING CHECKS:

DOES EMMET HAVE ENOUGH OF AN AVAILABLE BALANCE FOR THIS $4.75 PURCHASE?

IS THIS TRANSACTION WITHIN THE TRANSACTION AMOUNT LIMIT FOR THE DAY? FOR EXAMPLE, SOME ISSUERS MAY PREVENT SPEND OVER A CERTAIN DOLLAR AMOUNT.

IS EMMET ALLOWED TO SPEND AT THIS TYPE OF LOCATION? FOR EXAMPLE, SOME ISSUERS MAY PREVENT SPEND AT CERTAIN LOCATIONS. EACH MERCHANT LOCATION WILL HAVE A MERCHANT CATEGORY CODE (MCC), AND IF THE ISSUER BLACKLISTS A CERTAIN MCC, THEN THE TRANSACTION WILL BE DECLINED.

DOES THE TRANSACTION IN QUESTION TRIP ANY FRAUD ALERTS? THE ISSUER MAY HAVE CERTAIN RULES IN PLACE THAT COULD MARK A TRANSACTION AS FRAUDULENT AND THUS DECLINE THE TRANSACTION.

ONCE ALL OF THESE CHECKS PASS, THEN MONEYBIN BANK'S ISSUER PROCESSOR WILL SEND AN APPROVAL RESPONSE TO MASTERCARD.

THE ACQUIRER PROCESSOR THEN PASSES THE APPROVAL MESSAGE TO THE PAYMENT TERMINAL.

THE PAYMENT TERMINAL THEN SHOWS THE APPROVAL MESSAGE TO EMMET.

It seems simple, right? Well, actually, in the three seconds, a lot of things were going on. Emmet participated in a Dual-Message Signature transaction with his debit card. Referred to as a Dual-Message transaction or a Signature transaction because, typically, an Authorization (message One) happens at the time of swipe—which was the process discussed above. This is then followed up with a Clearing (message Two) that happens in bulk at the end of the night—which will be discussed in the following chapter. In some cases, the Authorization message (message one) can be different from the Clearing (message two) if a tip is included or some adjustment is made.

As you can see, a lot goes on within a very short period of time at the time of Authorization. In Emmet's scenario, it was a pretty basic check that can be done very quickly because the networks standardized on the ISO 8583 message. The ISO 8583 message is a very compact message and can travel quickly among the Payment Terminal, Acquirer Processor, Network, and the Issuer Processor.

The parties involved have all agreed to do their part within that three-second time window, and if responses are delayed, then that results in a poor experience for end cardholders such as Emmet, who won't be able to enjoy his Bucks of Star mocha.

While this is a basic use case, the Card Issuer may want to put in more sophisticated authorization rules, by looking at things such as geo-location, and can be managed by modern Issuer Processors like Marqeta. We'll discuss further authorization decision capabilities by looking at how a donut delivery company authorizes its own transactions in a later chapter.

KEY TAKEAWAYS
- The act of swiping, dipping, or tapping a card can enable you to buy things within seconds.
- The Authorization process places a hold on funds but doesn't actually move money at that very moment.

UP NEXT...
How does real money move from a cardholder's bank account to the Merchant's bank account?

CHAPTER 3

ANATOMY OF THE SWIPE PART 2: CLEARING AND SETTLEMENT

RECAP

In Anatomy of the Swipe Part 1, we learned:

- Bucks of Star Coffee has a Payment Terminal that communicates with its Merchant Acquirer and Acquirer Processor.
- Emmet has a Mastercard debit card that is issued by Moneybin Bank.
- When Emmet "dips" his Mastercard debit card into Bucks of Star Coffee's Payment Terminal, his purchase is approved within three seconds.

HOW DOES MONEY ACTUALLY MOVE FROM EMMET'S BANK ACCOUNT TO BUCKS OF STAR COFFEE'S BANK ACCOUNT?

The swipe of the card, referred to as the Authorization, typically puts a hold on funds in the cardholder's account. So, for example, if you look at any of your credit card or debit card online statements, you will see a section at the top of the screen showing "Pending Transactions." This is because the transaction hasn't officially cleared. In most cases, a transaction will clear the following day, but there could be other instances where it takes longer to clear. When the clearing transaction is presented and settlement happens, the funds are actually moved from your bank to the Merchant's bank.

> *Key Term: Clearing*
> *The term "Clearing" is used primarily by Issuers, but can also be referred to as "Capture" by Merchant Acquirers. Clearing happens toward the end of the day for most Merchants and will factor in tips, transaction reversals, and returns. This is basically the Merchant confirming these transactions are valid and that these funds are ready to be moved or "settled."*

> *Key Term: Settlement*
> *Settlement is the actual movement of money from the cardholder's bank account, the Issuing Bank, to the Merchant's bank account, the Acquiring Bank. This movement of money typically happens via Fedwire as instructed by the payment networks.*

AUTHORIZATION

AUTHORIZATION HAPPENS AT THE TIME OF SWIPE

Let's examine Emmet's mocha purchase at Bucks of Star Coffee. His coffee was $4.75, and he added a tip of $1. The Authorization transaction or the first part of the dual-message transaction was for $4.75 and that was approved before Emmet got his mocha. The Issuer Processor checked to make sure that he had at least $4.75 in his bank account.

CARDHOLDER'S AVAILABLE BALANCE GOES DOWN

Before Emmet ordered the mocha, he had exactly $1,000 in his Moneybin Bank checking account. At the time of Authorization, there was a funds hold placed on $4.75 out of $1,000, but at this time, the money hadn't moved. So, his actual bank balance remained at $1,000 until the transaction settled. However, his available balance will show up as $995.25. This means that if Emmet was to go out and try to purchase something for more than $995.25, the transaction would get declined because it exceeded his available balance.

PENDING TRANSACTIONS APPEAR AT TIME OF SWIPE ON THE CARDHOLDER'S ACCOUNT

In his Moneybin Bank mobile app, he'll be able to see a transaction for $4.75 at Bucks of Star Coffee as "Pending" on the day of the purchase.

CLEARING

MERCHANT "CLEARS" THE TRANSACTION AT END OF DAY

Toward the end of the day, Bucks of Star Coffee will submit a clearing file to the Network for settlement. Some payment terminals do this automatically, but with some payment terminals, this is a manual push of the button. Emmet's transaction will be submitted with the addition of the $1 tip. The clearing transaction sent will contain the breakdown of the actual authorized amount of the mocha and the tip amount. This second part of the Dual-Message transaction is referred to as clearing.

The second part of the message, or the clearing (also referred to as the capture), allows the Merchant to make adjustments to transactions before submitting to the card network. So, for example, if a customer is double charged, then the transaction can be voided before the movement of money happens as part of Settlement.

In the case of online transactions, clearing typically happens when goods are shipped. This is why you may see a transaction that you may have made online staying in a "Pending" state for a long period of time.

SETTLEMENT

TRANSACTIONS "SETTLE" THE FOLLOWING BUSINESS DAY

The following business day, the transaction "settles," and this transaction moves from the Pending category in Emmet's Moneybin Bank mobile app to the Completed transactions section. However, the amount will show the added tip of $1, so the transaction will actually show up as $5.75.

CARD HOLDER'S ACTUAL BALANCE GOES DOWN

- At Settlement, the original pending transaction of $4.75 for Emmet gets reversed, so he shouldn't see that transaction anymore as "Pending."
- He will now see a transaction of $5.75 ($4.75 + the $1.00 tip) in his completed transactions section.
- His available balance will be $994.25 ($1,000 beginning balance – $4.75 for the coffee – $1 tip).
- His actual balance will reflect the same $994.25 ($1,000 beginning balance – $4.75 for the coffee – $1 tip).
- At this point, Mastercard, via Fedwire, has moved the money out of Emmet's bank account and into the bank account of Bucks of Star Coffee's Merchant Acquirer.
- Bucks of Star Coffee's Merchant Acquirer then sends the money to Bucks of Star Coffee's bank account via Automated Clearing House (ACH).

NETWORK ASSESSES FEES FOR EACH TRANSACTION

During Settlement, the Card Network, Mastercard does not send Bucks of Star Coffee the full $5.75 for Emmet's coffee and tip. The Card Network will:

- Keep a percentage of the $5.75 for itself as the Network Assessment Fee.

- Take a percentage of the $5.75 and pass it on to the card Issuer as the Interchange Fee.

NETWORK SENDS A SETTLEMENT FILE TO THE ACQUIRER PROCESSOR AND ISSUER PROCESSOR

When this happens, Bucks of Star Coffee will know exactly how much money they will be credited from this transaction. Moneybin Bank, Emmet's Issuing Bank, will know exactly how much money will be debited from Emmet's account and how much revenue will be made from the Interchange fee.

INTERCHANGE/NETWORK ASSESSMENTS/ACQUIRER FEES ARE APPLIED

Transacting via debit or credit card doesn't cost Emmet anything. However, the Merchant is charged by the card network. So, in this case, Bucks of Star Coffee pays a few fees for this transaction that is netted out of the total transaction value of Emmet's mocha. This percentage varies greatly based on:

- Location
- Merchant Type
- Type of card you are using (credit versus debit, and even within these two types, is it a business card or a consumer card, or by card network tiers like "World" and "Platinum")
- Transaction mode (was it a signature transaction versus a Personal Identification Number (PIN) debit transaction and how the transaction was done [i.e., Was the chip used? Was it done online?])

These rules are all governed by very large rate tables that are set by the Card Networks; that is, these aren't things that are arbitrary or can be negotiated.

For the sake of simplicity, let's assume that the Interchange fee is 1 percent (this is a consumer debit card, transacting as a signature transaction at a Merchant type of "restaurant"). For Emmet's mocha, that would be about $0.06 ($5.75 x 0.01). Mastercard also takes a network assessment fee, and again for the sake of simplicity, let's assume that is also 1 percent, so another $0.06 ($5.75 x 0.01) for the Card Network.

Finally, the Merchant Acquirer charges an Acquirer fee to the Merchant. This typically is handled at the end of the month and could be a flat fee or a percentage.

FUNDS ARE SETTLED

When Mastercard, the Card Network, moves the money from Emmet's bank to Bucks of Star Coffee's Merchant Acquirer's bank, it does so like this:

- Debits Emmet's account for $5.75.
- Leaves $0.06 for Moneybin Bank because they are the Issuer of Emmet's debit card. This $0.06 is considered revenue for Moneybin Bank because they issued the card to Emmet.
- Keeps $0.06 Network Assessment fee for itself.
- Sends $5.63 (5.75 – 0.06 Network Assessment – 0.06 Interchange) to Bucks of Star Coffee's Merchant Acquirer's bank.

MONEY MOVES VIA FEDWIRE

This money is moved by Mastercard by using the Fedwire payments system that allows money movement from bank to bank. This money is pulled out of the Issuer's settlement bank account. This is done in aggregate, as there are probably more people than Emmet at Moneybin Bank buying things. Then, funds are pushed to the Merchant Acquirer's settlement account.

KEY TAKEAWAYS

- Money doesn't move at the time of swipe. It typically happens a day or two later.
- The cardholder doesn't pay any fees for the transaction.
- The Merchant pays a set of fees for the transaction.
- The fees being charged to the Merchant are netted out of the transaction amount paid out to the Merchant during settlement.
  - Network and Card Issuer Fees are moved at time of settlement.
  - The Merchant Acquirer in many cases collects their fee at the end of the month.

UP NEXT...

Let's examine what happens when a transaction has settled and needs to be disputed via a chargeback.

CHAPTER 4

ANATOMY OF THE SWIPE PART 3: CHARGEBACK

———

RECAP

In Anatomy of the Swipe Part 2, we learned:

- Toward the end of the business day, a Merchant will "clear" or "capture" the day's transactions and send it to the card networks for settlement. These amounts may include tips, and, thus, these amounts may be higher than the authorization amounts at the time of swipe.
- Money actually moves a day or two after the swipe has occurred.
- Settlement refers to the actual movement of money between the Issuing Bank and the Merchant Acquiring Bank.
- The Merchant pays a set of fees including the Network Assessment Fee, which goes to the card network, and the Interchange Fee, which goes to the Issuing Bank of the card.

- Transactions will move from a "pending" state to a "completed" state in a cardholder's bank account history. This indicates that money has been settled and moved out of the cardholder's bank (Issuing Bank) to the Merchant's bank (Acquiring Bank).

HAVE YOU EVER SEEN A TRANSACTION ON YOUR CARD STATEMENT THAT YOU DON'T RECOGNIZE?

This scenario has probably happened to most of us at least once. In many cases, it is a charge that you may not recognize because the name of the Merchant doesn't ring a bell, or perhaps you do recognize the name of the Merchant and you did not receive merchandise from them. Perhaps you received the merchandise from the Merchant, but it was faulty or not to your expectations, and now the Merchant isn't allowing a return. Consumers are protected by laws put in place by the Federal Reserve. More specifically, Regulation E for Debit Cards and Regulation Z for Credit Cards allow consumers to "Chargeback the Transaction."

> *Key Term: Chargeback*
> *When a cardholder doesn't recognize a charge on a credit or debit card, they may request their money back through their Issuing Bank. Chargebacks can also be used in case goods and services have not been provided by the Merchant, but the Merchant refuses to return the money. This step will happen after settlement.*

Here is a scenario that happened to Emmet:

1. Emmet also has a Visa credit card issued by Moneybin Bank that can work internationally and does not incur any foreign transaction fees. Emmet loves using this card because it is accepted everywhere and gives him some fairly decent cashback rewards. This is in addition to his Mastercard debit card also issued by Moneybin Bank.

2. Emmet is going on a business trip to Japan and decides to bring this credit card with him.

3. He is using this credit card to buy train tickets, food, souvenirs, and to enjoy fresh sushi from the Tskiji Fish Market.

4. As he is enjoying his sushi, he gets a push notification from his Moneybin Bank app that there has been a card transaction at Katy Spade for $535.86.

5. He checks the time back in the US and it is one o'clock in the morning.

6. He calls Moneybin Bank's cardholder support (listed on the back of his credit card issued by Moneybin Bank) and inquires about this charge because he is in Japan right now and did not make a purchase at Katy Spade, nor is this a typical type of purchase he would make.

7. After authenticating, the cardholder support rep looks at the transaction and determines that the transaction was made online, meaning that it wasn't a physical swipe at a retailer.

8. Emmet tries to recall if he had ordered something from Katy Spade and it may have just charged him when the product shipped.

9. Emmet was about to ask the cardholder support representative to mark this transaction as fraudulent, but then the representative asks if someone else could have made this purchase. Emmet has a secondary card that his wife uses.

10. Emmet sends a WhatsApp message to his wife asking if she made this purchase, although it was one o'clock in the morning back home and she should be fast asleep now.

11. No response from Emmet's wife because logically she should be asleep.

12. Emmet is now in a dilemma because if he marks this transaction as fraudulent, then he's going to need to get a brand-new card, and he needs this card to get him through the rest of the week before he gets back to the United States.

13. Emmet asks the representative if there is a way to just block transactions going forward on his card.

14. The representative shows him how to freeze his credit card within his Moneybin Bank mobile app.

15. Emmet goes into the Moneybin Bank mobile app and freezes his card.

16. Emmet takes a deep breath and then takes a bite out of his amazingly fresh fatty tuna sushi.

17. At the end of the meal, he gives his credit card to the waiter and unfreezes his card from his Moneybin Bank mobile app.

18. The transaction goes through, and he receives a push notification.

19. He then immediately freezes the card again.

20. Later in the evening, Emmet calls his wife and inquires about the Katy Spade charge. Luckily, it was a charge that she had made. The baby woke her up at one o'clock in the morning, and she couldn't go back to sleep so she decided to do some online shopping...

21. Luckily, for Emmet, this wasn't a fraudulent transaction and the crisis was averted.

ZERO LIABILITY POLICY

In the alternative case, if Emmet or his wife didn't make the purchase at Katy Spade, Emmet would qualify for Visa's Zero Liability policy. Since neither he nor his wife made the charge, they wouldn't have to pay for this and would get refunded. The cost to Emmet is that he's going to need to be reissued a new card with a new number and then he would need to go and update his streaming subscriptions, mobile phone bill, and a number of other recurring billers to have the new card number in addition to updating all of his online shopping websites the next time he shops there.

But what would have happened to the $535.86? Would Visa be paying for that? Well, not really, but this is what is commonly referred to as a Chargeback. This type of chargeback (a chargeback due to the cardholder thinking that their card was stolen), accounts for 30 percent of all chargebacks according to Chargebacks911 Chargeback Stats report.[5]

Who then is actually liable for paying for chargebacks if the cardholders fall into a Zero Liability policy set up by the card networks?

The Federal Trade Commission has set some policies for handling chargebacks on debit and credit cards,[6] but ultimately, it falls on the card Issuer to make a decision as to how much liability will actually fall on the cardholder. In Emmet's case, he's been a very loyal customer of Moneybin Bank. The bank

---

5   "Chargeback Stats," Chargebacks 911, accessed on January 26, 2020.
6   "Lost or Stolen Credit, ATM, and Debit Cards," Federal Trade Commission: Consumer Information, accessed on January 26, 2020.

may decide to cover the entire cost of this if the liability falls on the card Issuer and not the Merchant.

HOW THE CHARGEBACK IS PROCESSED

Key Term: EMV Chip Card

EMV originally stood for "Europay, Mastercard, Visa," which established the technical standard for encoding the card data onto a secure chip placed on a card. Cards with this type of chip and data encryption can be "dipped" into card terminals to pay for goods and services in a secure way. This method of storing card data is considered far more secure than data stored on the magnetic stripe on the back of a card used to "swipe." The EMV standard is now managed by EMVco, which is now a consortium of financial companies.

The rules are evolving around this, however, considering that Emmet was using an EMV Chip card, the flow would work like this:

1. Emmet would report the transaction as fraudulent to Moneybin Bank's cardholder support.
2. Moneybin Bank's cardholder support would freeze Emmet's card and reissue him a new card with a new card number.
3. Moneybin Bank, as the Card Issuer and the Issuing Bank, would file this chargeback with Visa, the Card Network.
4. Visa will then immediately send a credit transaction back to Emmet's card. This is referred to as a provisional credit.

5. Visa would take the money back immediately from Katy Spade because it was a "Card Not Present" transaction.
6. Visa would then send this transaction to Katy Spade to request some documentation.
7. Katy Spade has forty-five days to respond to the chargeback request.

DISPUTING THE CHARGEBACK

Katy Spade, the Merchant, can either dispute the chargeback or do nothing:

1. **Do nothing**—If Katy Spade does not respond within the forty-five-day window, then the chargeback case is closed, and Katy Spade would be paying for the chargeback. The Network assesses chargeback fees between $25 to $35 just to process the chargeback. This fee is applied regardless of if the chargeback is disputed or not. Had the amount been for less than that, it doesn't make sense for the Merchant to fight it because they would need to pay the chargeback fee regardless. Additionally, paperwork that the Merchant needs to provide to fight the claim is needed, such as a receipt proving that the user actually made the purchase and how it was purchased (online, in person, and if in person, then was the EMV Chip used or was the magnetic stripe used?). Some Merchants may just build in a threshold for certain types of chargebacks where it isn't worth fighting and bake it into their overall business model.

2. **Dispute**—If Katy Spade responds with a receipt and proof that Emmet did make the purchase, then the chargeback can be disputed.

a. The chargeback then goes into arbitration and this is where Moneybin Bank as the Issuer would then have to make the decision as to "eat the cost" or to pass it back on to Emmet. The good news for Emmet is that the Federal Trade Commission has capped the liability to the consumer to $50 for unauthorized spend on a credit card. The consumer liability is higher for debit cards if a card is reported lost and based on when the lost card was reported.

b. If Katy Spade is able to provide good documentation that this purchase was made by Emmet's card, but then we find out that Emmet's physical card was lost or stolen, then the card Issuer, Moneybin Bank, would be liable to eat this cost. In addition to the actual cost of the item, Moneybin Bank will also be charged a fee from the network in the range of $25 to $35.

EMV CHIP—MORE LIABILITY ON TO THE MERCHANT

With the advent of the EMV Chip card, even more scrutiny is placed on the Merchant. In physical locations, had this been a physical Katy Spade store, Visa would check to see if this transaction was done by using the EMV Chip or if it was swiped using the magnetic stripe across the top. In the United States, if an EMV Chip card is available, and the Merchant does not use the chip and instead swipes using the magnetic stripe, the chargeback liability immediately goes to the Merchant and the Merchant will not be able to fight it. This is how the card networks have been able to mandate that new payment terminals be rolled out that can accept EMV-Chip-based transactions. The reason for this is that the EMV Chip is far more secure than the magnetic stripe. It isn't so easy for card thieves to install a "card-skimmer" device that can read the card data off of the EMV Chip.

ONLINE TRANSACTIONS—DIFFERENT LIABILITY RULES

For online transactions like this one, since you can't physically insert the EMV Chip into the card reader (referred to as a "Card Not Present" transaction), Visa will check that the card number was entered with the Card Verification Value (CVV) code (three-digit code on the back). If we find that the CVV was missing, this could also put the Merchant at risk for paying for this chargeback.

3D SECURE

Key Term: 3D Secure
This is a standard for offering cardholders one more layer of security for online transactions. When card numbers are entered into a website to pay for something, 3D Secure will require the cardholder to enter one more form of authentication, such as a one-time-use PIN or passcode, similar to how two-factor authentication works for websites.

More recently, the card networks are requiring Merchants and card Issuers to roll out a service called 3D Secure. The technology is standard in Europe but not yet in the US. With this technology, online Merchants may require a second authentication method to process the transaction. With earlier versions of this, at the time of checkout, a text message would be sent to the cardholder after an online transaction, then they would need to respond back to the text message with a "Yes" to confirm the transaction, or the cardholder would receive a PIN code that they would then need to key into their browser to complete the transaction. The user gets a few minutes to respond to this before the transaction is canceled.

In newer versions of 3D Secure, the card Issuer can build it into their mobile or web interfaces, where a push notification is triggered, and then the user would go and tap that notification and be directed to their mobile app. In the mobile app, they would then be able to select yes or no if they made that transaction.

3D SECURE 1.0

This is how earlier implementations of 3D Secure operate:

1. Emmet makes a purchase online and proceeds to checkout.
2. After adding his card to the online portal, he receives a pop-up that requests a PIN code to be entered in (there is usually a time-out of five minutes—so if Emmet doesn't respond within that time with the right PIN code, then the transaction won't go through).
3. Emmet checks his phone and there is a text message with a PIN code in it.
4. He types that PIN code into the browser pop-up.
5. The transaction goes through and the online web Merchant shows a confirmation screen of the order and sends an email receipt to Emmet.

3D SECURE 2.0

This is how newer implementations of 3D Secure operate:

1. Emmet makes a purchase online and proceeds to checkout.
2. After adding his card to the online portal, he receives a pop-up that requests approval through his banking app (there is usually a time-out of five minutes—so if Emmet doesn't respond by taking action in his app, then the transaction won't go through).
3. Emmet gets a push notification on his phone to approve his online transaction.
4. Emmet taps on the push notification that brings him to an approval screen in his Moneybin Bank mobile app.
5. The transaction amount and Merchant name appear with a button to approve the transaction.
6. Emmet presses the approve button in his Moneybin Bank mobile app.
7. The transaction goes through and the online web Merchant shows a confirmation screen of the order and sends an email receipt to Emmet.

CALCULATING CHARGEBACK RATES

Merchants will typically want to keep their chargeback rates below 1 percent. Once a Merchant gets close to 1 percent or goes over, it needs to work to bring that percentage down or risk losing their ability to accept card-based payments through their Merchant Acquirer. The card networks place stringent rules on their Merchant Acquirers to make sure that all Merchants maintain chargeback rates below 1 percent. Specialized Merchant Acquirers will underwrite riskier businesses but will charge a lot more per transaction.

Chargeback rate is calculated by taking the total number of chargeback transactions in a month and dividing it by the total number of transactions in a month. Depending on the type of business, the percentage could vary significantly; however, it should be below 1 percent to be in good standing.

PREVENTING CHARGEBACKS

While certain types of fraudulent transactions are unavoidable, having a good return policy and collecting more information about the consumer upfront will help reduce chargebacks.

For online transactions, asking the consumer to enter their CVV number during checkout and asking for their billing address can help prevent fraudulent transactions upfront.

For in-person transactions, asking the consumer to transact with their EMV Chip will help reduce the chargeback burden on the Merchant.

KEY TAKEAWAYS

- Consumers are protected from fraudulent transactions because of consumer protection laws. The Networks reinforce this because they want consumers to feel secure in using their credit or debit cards for their purchases.
- The card networks have implemented "Zero Liability" policies for their cardholders to help ease consumer concerns that card transactions "aren't safe."

- The chargeback is paid for by the Merchant or the Card Issuer. Visa or Mastercard do not pay for these chargebacks directly.
- The Burden of Proof always falls on to the Merchant. They can choose to fight the chargeback by providing additional documentation.
- If the Merchant can provide proof of the transaction, then it is up to the card Issuer to request further documentation from the cardholder or just "eat the cost."
- Newer technologies such as the EMV Chip and 3D Secure are giving more tools to Merchants to help prevent chargebacks. If the transaction was processed correctly by using these new technologies, the Merchant typically doesn't end up paying for the chargeback.

UP NEXT...

A deeper look into the card networks and how they operate within the payments ecosystem.

PART 2

PAYMENTS ECOSYSTEM

CHAPTER 5

PAYMENTS ECOSYSTEM PART 1: CARD NETWORKS

WHAT ARE THE CARD NETWORKS AND WHAT IS THEIR ROLE?

At the heart of every card swipe is the Card Network, sometimes also referred to as a Card Scheme. The major Card

Networks in the US are Visa, Mastercard, American Express, and Discover. China has China Unionpay, Japan has Japan Credit Bureau (JCB), and while not considered Card Networks, Alipay and PayPal are, in fact, a type of payment network. For the sake of this chapter, we will be excluding Alipay and PayPal as examples.

The Card Network's job is to pass information from the Merchant Acquirer to the Issuer and vice-versa. The Card Networks set the rules for both Merchant Acquirers and Issuers. It sets the format for communicating (ISO8583 protocol) and also sets the rules for disputes so that disagreements are all handled in the same way. When these rules are adhered to, they provide a license to use their brand to Issuing Banks and Acquiring Banks.

OPEN VERSUS CLOSED CARD NETWORKS

Visa and Mastercard are considered open Card Networks, whereas Discover and American Express are closed Card Networks.

VISA AND MASTERCARD: OPEN CARD NETWORKS

The key difference is that Visa and Mastercard will have relationships with multiple Merchant Acquirers and multiple Issuers. They typically don't play any favorites and like to work in more of a marketplace function. This is why these Card Networks will typically invest in Issuers and Acquirers, but they won't actually purchase these players.

AMERICAN EXPRESS AND DISCOVER: CLOSED CARD NETWORKS

American Express and Discover typically issue their own cards, are their own bank, and typically provide their own acquiring services. This level of control affords Discover and American Express to control and own Interchange revenue, Card Network revenue, and Acquirer revenue.

HOW DO VISA AND MASTERCARD MAKE MONEY?

In the case of Visa and Mastercard, because they sit in the middle, they are able to collect money from the Merchants and Issuers. Here is how Visa and Mastercard make their money:

FEES ASSESSED TO THE MERCHANT

When a card that is issued by Moneybin Bank is swiped at Bucks of Star Coffee, Bucks of Star Coffee is charged the following fees:

FEES ASSESSED TO THE ISSUER

The card Issuer, Moneybin Bank, is charged the following fees:

- After the transaction has cleared, a reporting settlement fee is typically charged to the Issuer from the Card Network; this is typically a flat fee per transaction.
- The Card Network will also charge the Issuer a per-transaction fee that is assessed on the authorization transaction and the clearing transaction. Another way to think about this is that the Issuer is assessed a usage fee for transmitting data through the Card Network's "rails."
- There are other Software-as-a-Service-type fees charged to the Issuer like fraud services and settlement services.

ACQUIRERS AND ISSUERS ARE THE DISTRIBUTORS OF VISA AND MASTERCARD

Visa and Mastercard's strategy is about getting as many cards out there as possible and making sure these cards are accepted in as many places as possible. Another good way to think about it is that the Acquirers and Issuers are marketing vehicles and distributors for the Card Networks or card brands. The Issuers are responsible for getting more cards in the hands of users, and the Acquirers are responsible for getting as many card terminals and payment gateways in the hands of Merchants so they can accept card payments.

HOW DO AMERICAN EXPRESS AND DISCOVER MAKE MONEY?

In the context of Discover and American Express, in most cases, these Card Networks are able to take the Interchange, Acquirer Fee, and Network Assessment. They are able to do this because they are also issuing their own cards and providing acquiring services. Because of this, they can adjust these fees depending on the size of the Merchant but also, their revenue per swipe is significantly higher than Visa and Mastercard.

However, their total swipe volume is significantly lower than Visa and Mastercard because they don't have a network of Issuers and Acquirers getting their cards or card terminals into the market on their behalf. As a good frame of reference, in 2017, Visa accounted for 60 percent of all purchase volume in the US for all debit and credit cards. American Express only accounted for 13 percent, and Discover was at 2 percent.[7]

CARD NETWORK RAILS AND TRANSACTION ROUTING

In the background, all transactions are routed through some Card Network "rail." Depending on how the cardholder swiped their card, the Card Network rail is determined. Three types of Card Network rails exist:

---

7   "Payment Cards in Circulation Worldwide - Projected," Nilson Research, October 2019, Issue 1162, accessed on January 26, 2020.

CREDIT NETWORKS (DUAL MESSAGE)

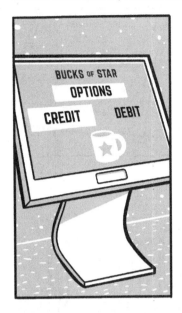

The typical mode of operating for these card networks is via the "Credit Network." Sometimes, when you go to make a swipe at a card terminal, it will ask you if you want to use "Credit" or "Debit." In most cases, you will select "Credit" if you have a credit card, and you can also select this if you have a debit card. The key difference to the cardholder is that if you select "Credit," you may need to sign for the purchase, whereas if you select "Debit" then you will need to put in your four-digit PIN. However, under the hood, by selecting "Credit," your card will actually charge the Merchant a higher Interchange rate. If you select "Debit," the Merchant will be charged a lower Interchange rate. This transaction mode is also referred to as a "Signature Purchase."

THE TWO PARTS OF THE DUAL-MESSAGE SWIPE

The first part of the "Dual Message" is the Authorization, which effectively holds funds on the cardholder's account until the transaction clears. The clearing transaction (typically occurs the following day) is the second part of the "Dual Message," and this is where the money is actually removed from the cardholder's account. If a tip is added, then it will appear in the clearing transaction.

PIN DEBIT NETWORKS (SINGLE MESSAGE)

For debit cards, each Card Network has a secondary network brand for PIN Debit or Automated Teller Machine (ATM). This mode typically yields a much lower Interchange. So, if you are using a Visa debit card from Bank of America, when it runs on the VisaNet "Credit" network, the Interchange is higher, whereas, in the "Debit" mode running on the Interlink network, the Interchange will be lower. This transaction mode is also referred to as a "PIN Debit Purchase." When the cardholder selects this mode, they will be prompted to enter their four-digit PIN, and then the transaction will complete.

Since this is considered a "Single-Message" transaction, there isn't a distinct authorization transaction followed by a clearing transaction like in a Dual-Message transaction. All of it happens in one transaction, meaning that the cardholder's available balance and actual balance are reduced at the same time. The concept of "holding funds" does not exist in this transaction.

The PIN Debit networks are as follows:

	Visa	Mastercard	Discover
PIN Debit Network	– Interlink – VisaNet Debit	Maestro	Pulse

ATM NETWORKS

Taking money off of a debit card actually works the inverse of a typical card swipe. Here is a breakdown of fees charged by an ATM:

The ATM will charge the user a flat fee, typically around $3. If the ATM is included in your bank's network, like if you bank with Wells Fargo and you go to a Wells Fargo ATM, then this fee is waived. However, if you bank with Wells Fargo and you use a Bank of America ATM, you will be charged around $3. So, if you need $20, then it will remove $23 from your bank account and give you $20 cash.

Additionally, the Issuer of the card is charged an Interchange fee by the ATM (sometimes referred to as reverse-Interchange), which is counter to how a swipe transaction would work at the register. This is typically a percentage of the transaction. This is why most card Issuers will encourage their users to use ATMs within their network.

The reason why you can take money out of just about any ATM is because of the Durbin Amendment and its requirement that every debit card must have a secondary unaffiliated network. This law was put in to give consumers more choice in finding an ATM network. For example, if you have a debit card from Visa and the ATM doesn't support Visa's ATM networks, then it can run on Mastercard's ATM network, Cirrus.

ATM transactions follow a pattern similar to a Single-Message transaction in that everything happens as one single transaction and the cardholder's available balance and actual balance are reduced at the same time. The concept of "holding funds" does not exist in this transaction.

The ATM networks are as follows:

	Visa	Mastercard	Discover
ATM Network	Plus	Cirrus	Pulse

FREE ATM NETWORKS

Two major ATM Networks, MoneyPass (32,000 ATMs in the US), and Allpoint (45,000 ATMs in the US) have a network of ATMs throughout the US that are "Free" to end-users if that Issuer offers either of these two networks. Many of the neo-banks (online only banks), such as Branch, Chime, Money Lion, and Varo offer access to these networks. In this case, the end-user of their debit card could go to these ATMs and take money out without incurring any fees. These fees, however, are passed on to the card Issuer, so in effect, Chime is paying for these ATM withdrawals. Both of these networks have ATM locators, and in the case of Allpoint, many of their terminals are inside of Target, CVS, and Walgreens stores.

KEY TAKEAWAYS

- The Card Networks serve as the "rails" that the card-based transaction will travel on. The Card Networks pass data between Acquirers and Issuers to ensure the transaction completes on these "rails."
- The Card Networks establish the rules for the ecosystem.
- Visa and Mastercard are considered "Open Card Networks," while Discover and American Express are

considered "Closed Card Networks." Visa and Mastercard rely heavily on their network of Acquirers and Issuers to distribute their brands out into the market. Discover and American Express control their ecosystem and take on the role of distribution by themselves.

- Visa and Mastercard are able to charge Merchants and Issuers via different fees.
- The card networks have subnetworks to facilitate credit, debit, and ATM transactions.

UP NEXT...

Let's understand why banks are a critical component to the payments ecosystem, and what it takes to build a bank.

CHAPTER 6

PAYMENTS ECOSYSTEM PART 2: BANKS

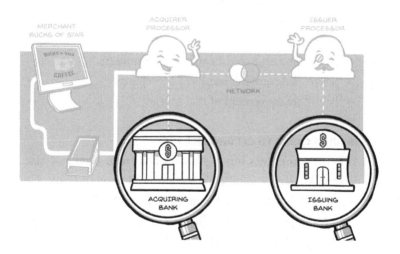

RECAP

In Payments Ecosystem Part 1, we learned:

- Visa and Mastercard are considered open card networks and can work with many Issuing and Acquiring banks.

They also work with many Issuer processors and Acquirer processors.

- American Express and Discover are considered closed card networks, and typically do their own processing and have their own banks.
- The card networks route transaction traffic between the Acquirer processors and Issuer processors. For this, they charge the Merchant a Network Assessment fee, and they charge the Acquirers and Issuers per-transaction fees.

WHAT IS THE ROLE OF BANKS IN THE PAYMENTS ECOSYSTEM?

In addition to the card networks, one of the critical components for the payments ecosystem to work are banks. Banks serve three primary functions:

- Issue debit and credit cards to cardholders
- Serve as Acquiring Banks to Merchants
- Facilitate movement of real money

ISSUING CARDS TO CARDHOLDERS

When Emmet was buying his mocha from Bucks of Star Coffee, he used a debit card issued by Moneybin Bank. He received this debit card by opening up a checking account with Moneybin Bank. He did so by confirming his identity by going through Moneybin Bank's Know Your Customer (KYC) process and passed screening from the Office of Foreign Assets Control (OFAC). By issuing a card to Emmet, the bank is underwriting Emmet.

SPONSORING A BIN

Only banks are allowed to issue cards for open card networks, such as Visa and Mastercard. It is important to understand that the open card networks, Visa and Mastercard, are not banks, they provide the infrastructure to transact with debit and credit cards. In effect, Visa and Mastercard are providing banks with a license to use their infrastructure. Alternatively, Discover and American Express will issue their own cards in most cases and will not issue through third-party banks.

Each card (debit or credit) has a six-digit Bank Identification Number (BIN), which is offered by Visa or Mastercard to a bank. The bank then issues the card to the cardholder. The Bank may or may not have their logo on the card, but it will usually have its name somewhere in the fine print on the back of every card they issue. If you look at the back of any debit or credit card, you will see a statement similar to this:

"This card is issued by <Bank Name>, pursuant to a license from <Visa or Mastercard>."

SERVE AS THE ACQUIRING BANK FOR MERCHANTS

When Bucks of Star Coffee received payment from Emmet's bank, Moneybin Bank, those funds were deposited into a bank account at Bucks of Star Coffee's Acquiring bank. An Acquiring bank performs various checks on the Merchant to verify that they are a legitimate business and the funds being received through card-based payments are truly for goods or services being sold by the Merchant.

FACILITATE MOVEMENT OF REAL MONEY

It is important to understand that money actually isn't being moved at the time of the card swipe. The real money moves at the time of settlement, typically a day later, and this movement of money happens between banks. In the US, the only entities that can actually move real money are banks or entities with money transmitter licenses.

BUILDING A BANK

With five million users banking with Chime, it is becoming very apparent that people are shifting their banking relationships away from the traditional banks like Wells Fargo, Bank of America, and Chase, to these new "Challenger Banks" or "Neo-Banks." In fact, according to CNBC,[8] Chime attracted four million of these users in the last year, showcasing an accelerated interest in the public toward neo-banks. According to Marqeta's Consumer Behavior Survey conducted in February of 2019,[9] millennials are preferring the mobile-first banking experiences that these neo-banks can offer and are tired of the monthly fees or overdraft fees that traditional banks put on these users.

Branch, Chime, MoneyLion, Varo, N26, Monzo, Revolut, and Current are just a few examples of neo-banks. These neo-banks are touting $0 fee banking, with no minimum account balance or deposit requirements. They also offer access to large networks of ATMs all for free.

---

8   Hugh Son, "This branchless bank quadrupled its customer base to 4 million in a single year," CNBC, accessed on January 26, 2020.

9   "Marqeta Consumer Behavior Survey," Marqeta, February, 2019, accessed on January 26, 2020.

But how are these neo-banks able to offer this while the big banks can't?

The main reason is that these new "neo-banks" aren't actually banks but rather tech companies that partner with regional banks such as Sutton Bank, Bancorp, or Meta Bank. These regional banks have less than $10 billion in assets and are able to charge a higher Interchange rate because they are considered exempt from the Interchange rules set forth in the Durbin Amendment and are considered "unregulated." This means that these regional banks are able to issue cards that earn higher "unregulated" Interchange. Instead of making their money from monthly account maintenance fees or overdraft fees, these challenger banks make their money from interest on the deposits and debit card Interchange.

UNREGULATED VERSUS REGULATED INTERCHANGE

BIG BANKS = REGULATED INTERCHANGE = LOWER INTERCHANGE

The big banks with larger asset sizes (higher deposit volume) are subject to the Durbin Amendment, part of the Dodd-Frank law. This law stipulates that banks with assets higher than $10 billion may not charge Interchange higher than 21 cents plus 0.05 percent (five Basis Points) x the value of the purchase. These banks fall into what is referred to as "Regulated Interchange."

SMALLER BANKS = UNREGULATED INTERCHANGE = HIGHER INTERCHANGE

Banks with assets less than $10 billion qualify for "Unregulated Interchange," and are able to charge higher Interchange rates for purchases.

GETTING A NATIONAL BANK CHARTER

Varo Money recently got preliminary approval for a National Bank Charter from the Office of the Comptroller of the Currency (OCC), which made history as Varo Money is the neo-bank to get this license. Varo currently offers checking accounts through The Bancorp Bank, but once the banking charter is fully approved, Varo will be able to offer checking accounts directly. This will enable Varo to have greater ability to control banking overhead costs but will need to build full banking operations to maintain compliance that previously was being provided by The Bancorp Bank.

FOUNDER STORY: ZACH PERRET: DEMOCRATIZING BANKING DATA FOR CONSUMERS WITH PLAID

Banks hold a treasure trove of data about you. Every check written to your landlord, every check deposited from your grandma, every paycheck deposited via direct deposit from your employer, every swipe of the debit card at your favorite retailers, every energy bill paid through the bank and every cable bill paid via the cable company's website, all appear within a bank's web portal or mobile app. You can also get your banking history by pulling bank statements online or perhaps you get them monthly in the mail.

The challenge has always been how you can use that data to build your own budget, get a mortgage, qualify for other loans, or just be able to get a pay advance on your earned wages, without downloading and sending your monthly statements so that some person on the other end can manually evaluate it. Additionally, if you ever needed to move money in or out of your bank account via ACH, you would need to carry around a checkbook with your account and routing number on it.

This is the problem that Zach Perret saw in 2013. He wanted to build a personal financial management mobile app because he saw that understanding their finances was the biggest cause of user distress. He found that without access to good banking data that is updated frequently, his mobile app wasn't entirely useful. He set out to find a way to easily connect to his bank's data and couldn't find a good way to do it, so he started building connectors that could surface his banking data through a mobile app. Moreover, he realized that people do remember their banking app's username and password, but they wouldn't be able to recall their account and routing number without having to pull it off of a paper check. Wouldn't it be great if his bank data could be exposed to the personal financial management mobile app he was building simply by providing his banking username and password?

As he was doing this, he realized that there were plenty of other software developers looking to access this banking data to build out other unique financial services. The problem was that getting to the financial data within banks was incredibly difficult to do. Most banks don't have Application Program Interfaces (APIs) that can allow developers easy access to the data, and none of the big banks are "in the cloud." He decided to take the difficult path and begin building these interfaces or "plumbing" to make this data available to other developers. This was the genesis of his company, Plaid, which now connects with over 11,000 financial institutions in the United States and Canada, and powers over 2,000 financial apps by software developers.

Fundamentally, Plaid is democratizing banking data for the banking customer/mobile app user. If you want to apply for a mortgage and you really don't want to pull together three years of account statements, you could authorize a mobile mortgage app to access your banking history via Plaid. After you download the mobile mortgage app, you would sign into your bank account using your bank login and password, and the relevant transaction history would be made available to the mobile mortgage app, which can then quickly tell you if you are qualified for a mortgage.

Additionally, if you wanted to move funds out of your Venmo mobile wallet to your bank account, you can also log in with your bank's login and password to enable an ACH transfer. You can do this without ever keying in your bank routing and account numbers. All of this can be done seamlessly through Plaid.

KEY TAKEAWAYS
- Only banks are allowed to Issue cards to cardholders.
- Banks underwrite Merchants and allow them to accept card-based payments.

- Banks facilitate the movement of real money during a card-based transaction.
- Challenger Banks or Neo-Banks such as Branch, Chime, MoneyLion, N26, and Revolut, aren't actually banks but rather they are tech companies that partner with banks.

UP NEXT...

Let's figure out how to accept card-based payments by using Acquiring Banks, Acquirer Processors, Payment Service Providers (PSPs), and Payment Facilitators (PayFacs).

CHAPTER 7

PAYMENTS ECOSYSTEM PART 3: TAKING PAYMENTS

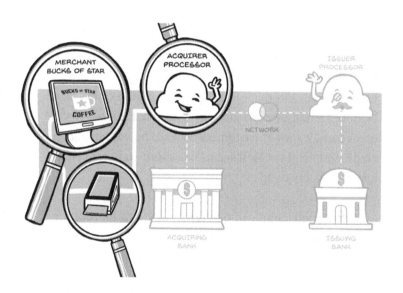

RECAP

In Payments Ecosystem Part 2, we learned:

- Banks underwrite Merchants and allow them to accept card-based payments.
- Banks facilitate the movement of real money from a cardholder's bank account at the Issuing Bank to the Merchant's bank account at the Acquiring Bank through the settlement process.

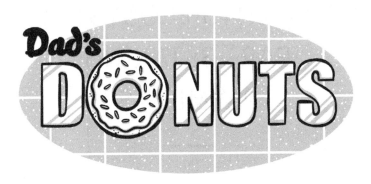

HOW CAN A MERCHANT START ACCEPTING CARD-BASED PAYMENTS?

Emmet's dad, Mufasa, opens up a donut shop called Dad's Donuts. Initially, he was just taking cash but realizes that he turned away a lot of customers because he couldn't accept credit and debit cards. It seems like more and more people just don't carry cash!

Mufasa started looking into different solutions for accepting credit cards and saw a few options:

USE AN ISO OR MERCHANT ACQUIRER DIRECTLY

Mufasa could work directly with a Merchant Acquirer, such as Wells Fargo, to get a Merchant Account. If Mufasa doesn't have a direct relationship with a Merchant Acquirer, such as Wells Fargo, he could go through an Independent Sales Organization (ISO) to establish this relationship. The Merchant Acquirer, in this case, Wells Fargo, then offers point-of-sale devices to accept card-based payments through its partners such as First Data. Going with a Merchant Acquirer directly will take a little more onboarding time but will provide a wider range of choice of hardware and software for the Merchant.

> *Key Term: Independent Sales Organization (ISO)*
> *An ISO is granted a license to sell Merchant acquiring services from a Merchant Acquirer such as Wells Fargo or Chase Paymentech.*

USE A PAYMENTS FACILITATOR

Another option, since he is just starting his business, is to work with a payments facilitator (sometimes referred to as a PF or PayFac) like Square or Toast to open a sub-Merchant account and get the point-of-sale device directly through them.

> *Key Term: Payments Facilitator (PF or PayFac)*
> *This is a layer on top of a Merchant Acquirer. Payments Facilitators can typically onboard Merchants very quickly and offer out-of-the-box hardware and software to enable a Merchant to start accepting card-based payments quickly.*

DONUT SHOP IS JUST GETTING GOING: USE A PAYMENTS FACILITATOR

Mufasa has been making donuts for years using his mother's recipes but only recently had the courage to open up a real donut shop. As with many entrepreneurs, there is a lot of uncertainty in if customers will like his donuts and whether he will be able to earn enough income to support himself and his business. Mufasa knows that customers are willing to pay him, but he doesn't have enough history as a business to open up a Merchant Account directly with a Merchant Acquirer. This is why Mufasa opts to get a payments solution from Square, a Payments Facilitator.

BENEFITS OF USING A PAYMENTS FACILITATOR

COOL HARDWARE

Mufasa really likes the option from Square because his cash register was pretty clunky, and he wasn't able to customize it. Square's register is able to accept card payments and also cash payments. Another benefit is that it can accept payments from Apple Pay and Google Pay, which he knows his customers like using.

FAST SETUP

Additionally, the setup process for Square is really easy. He set up an account within minutes by providing Square some information online. This can be done because Mufasa's donut shop would be considered a sub-Merchant under Square.

FIXED PRICING

He also saw that the pricing with Square was very simple, every swipe, dip, or tap would cost him 2.6 percent plus 10 cents regardless of if it was a debit card or credit card. This way, he can factor that cost into each donut. This is referred to as fixed pricing.

MANAGED FRAUD

When a customer sees a transaction that looks inaccurate, they will often call their Issuing Bank to get money back; this is referred to as a chargeback. In this scenario, Mufasa doesn't have to worry about a chargeback because the Payments Facilitator will provide Mufasa with tools to combat these chargebacks. Mufasa doesn't need to do any direct follow-up with Visa or Mastercard or the customer in this scenario.

OTHER SERVICES HIS BUSINESS NEEDS

In addition to accepting card-based payments, many Payments Facilitators offer other services and products that are specific to the company. Small retail businesses and restaurants like Mufasa's donut shop need things that can help manage their inventory, offer receipts to their customers, and allow them to add new SKUs to sell.

Mufasa will also want some analytics that can tell him what his best-sellers are and times of heavy traffic in his store so he can staff it accordingly.

DRAWBACKS OF USING A PAYMENTS FACILITATOR

BEING A SUB-MERCHANT

While from the get-go, this didn't matter so much to Mufasa, his donut shop is actually considered a sub-Merchant. Square is considered the main Merchant and already works with several Acquirers and banks to build a set of Merchant types. Mufasa's business fell into the "Restaurants" category. Because Square services so many restaurants, this was a very easy business for Square to underwrite. The drawback here is that anytime someone swipes a card at Mufasa's donut shop, the transaction history at the customer's bank will always start with an "SQ*."

FIXED PRICING CAN BE EXPENSIVE IN THE LONG HAUL

While the pricing was very transparent with Square, it was a bit pricier than some of the other options out there. Had Mufasa gone with a Merchant Acquirer directly, his cost would go down over time as he sells more donuts.

POTENTIAL FUNDS SETTLEMENT DELAY

If a customer buys a donut from Mufasa today (time = t), the network typically clears the transaction the following day (t+1). When this happens, funds settle with Square's bank tomorrow (t+1), and then Square will perform a calculation taking their 2.6 percent plus 10 cents out of the transaction and then send the funds to Mufasa's account at Square. If Mufasa would like these funds to go to his Wells Fargo bank account, then Square will send an ACH of this to Wells Fargo, which could take at least another day if not more (t+2).

HOW DO PAYMENTS FACILITATORS MAKE MONEY?

Most Payments Facilitators make money in two ways:

REVENUE FROM SOFTWARE OR HARDWARE

Because most Payments Facilitators offer their own hardware, they make money off of the initial sale or sometimes lease the hardware. In addition to that, Payments Facilitators like Square and Toast offer other software and services like inventory management, payroll, and scheduling software. Additionally, Merchants can take working capital loans from some Payments Facilitators.

REVENUE FROM EACH TRANSACTION

The major revenue source for most Payments Facilitators is the per-transaction fee. To make things simple for Merchants, Payments Facilitators typically charge a flat fee regardless of the type of card (in Mufasa's case, he's paying per swipe 2.6 percent plus 10 cents). On the back end, the Payments Facilitators are paying the card Issuers Interchange and the network's network assessment fees. Additionally, they are paying their Merchant Acquirer the Acquirer fee. Because the Payments Facilitator is underwriting multiple Merchants under them as sub-Merchants, the transaction volume from all sub-Merchants is aggregated for the Payments Facilitator. With higher transaction volume, the Payments Facilitator is able to negotiate very low Acquirer fees.

The flat transaction fee that is charged to the sub-Merchants in most cases is higher than what the Payments Facilitator pays in Acquirer fees, Interchange, and network assessments, which is where they make their margin.

DONUT SHOP EXPERIENCES EXPLOSIVE GROWTH: MOVING TO A MERCHANT ACQUIRER

Mufasa's donuts became a huge hit, with a line that forms around the building in the mornings. He quickly realizes that he has passed $500k in annual transaction volume. That's a lot of donuts! He has a conversation with his Square rep and they determine it may make sense for Mufasa to set up a direct Merchant Account. He now has to see what the benefits and drawbacks are of opening up a direct Merchant Account through a Merchant Acquirer.

BENEFITS OF USING A MERCHANT ACQUIRER

BEING A DIRECT MERCHANT

As a direct Merchant, Mufasa would be able to show the name of his donut shop in the transaction history of his customers' accounts. There wouldn't be an "SQ*" added to the front of the transaction as there would as a sub-merchant. He also would be able to control the exact Merchant Category Code associated with his business, which could help lower his Interchange rate.

He also won't have a top limit of dollars he can transact within a year, which opens him up for growth. This is typically $500k for Payments Facilitators under the sub-merchant arrangement.

HARDWARE AND SOFTWARE OPTIONS

Mufasa's can still use Square's hardware and software, but if he wanted to, he could choose other products to help him manage his payments, inventory, and accounting.

INTERCHANGE PLUS PRICING

By using a Merchant Acquirer directly, Mufasa has the option to use flat pricing as he had with Square or choose Interchange Plus pricing.

Interchange Plus works much like Emmet's mocha example, where each swipe would incur an Interchange fee that would be a percent of the total transaction, a Network Assessment fee that is typically percentage based, and then an Acquirer fee that can be a percentage or a flat amount per transaction. Based on Mufasa's donut shop's Merchant Category Code and the type of card his customers use, Interchange Plus pricing could vary dramatically for each transaction, but overall, his costs should go down because he is doing some serious volume!

Typically, the Acquirer fee can be set up on volume tiers, meaning that this cost could go down based on the total monthly volume at Mufasa's donut shop.

FASTER FUNDS SETTLEMENT

With a direct Merchant account, Mufasa would set up a bank account with the Merchant Acquirer. Funds would settle with the network directly. Visa and Mastercard will take out any network assessment and Interchange from the transaction and leave the remainder for Mufasa's donut shop. For example, if a customer buys a donut today, then funds will settle tomorrow in Mufasa's bank account. The additional step of moving the funds to Mufasa's Wells Fargo account via ACH is not needed.

The Merchant Acquirer would then bill Mufasa for their Acquirer fees at the end of the month or some pre-defined interval.

DRAWBACKS OF USING A MERCHANT ACQUIRER

MORE PAPERWORK
Establishing a direct Merchant account typically requires a lot of paperwork, including things such as incorporation papers, audited financial statements, certificates of good standing, and so on. For Mufasa who just started his donut shop, he typically will not have all of this information.

MANAGE HIS OWN FRAUD
In this model, Mufasa would need to manage his own fraud. He would use the tools provided to him via his Merchant Acquirer to do this, but ultimately, he's responsible for controlling this fraud and making sure his chargeback rates are at a controlled level.

HOW DO MERCHANT ACQUIRERS MAKE MONEY?
Most Merchant Acquirers make money in two ways:

REVENUE FROM HARDWARE

Since the primary focus of a Merchant Acquirer is to process transactions, its software and services are limited. They may have reseller agreements with point-of-sale manufacturers like Vantiv and First Data, where they would earn some commission. Alternatively, they could have their own hardware, where they would make a margin off of the hardware itself.

For some of the newer point-of-sale systems, they may have an app store where third-party developers can build apps. They could earn money from the app developers as well.

REVENUE FROM EACH TRANSACTION

Most Merchant Acquirers are also Acquirer Processors, meaning that they have a direct connection with the card networks such as Visa and Mastercard. An Acquirer Processor has hardware from Visa and Mastercard in its data centers to process the transactions. This hardware needs to be connected to a very fast network connection so that transactions can be relayed from the point-of-sale terminal to the card Networks and then to the card Issuer and back in less than three seconds.

For this processing capability, the Merchant Acquirer is able to charge the Merchant an Acquirer fee, which is typically a flat fee or a percentage for every transaction. They may also assess fees when cards are declined or when a chargeback happens.

The Merchant Acquirer takes the Interchange from the transaction and sends it to the Issuer, and sends the network assessment to the network, so this is not considered revenue for them.

DONUT SHOP GETS LARGE ORDERS FROM GROCERY STORES: ENTER THE PAYMENT SERVICE PROVIDER

Mufasa's magical donuts catch the attention of large grocery chains who want to offer his donuts at their retail locations. The grocery buyers want a place where they can put their orders in online and make payments on a monthly basis. This catches Mufasa by surprise because now he will need to open up a location just to service these large orders. Additionally, he doesn't have the cash flow to allow for "net 30" payment terms. So, he starts looking at potential solutions.

Mufasa didn't even have a website, so he sets up a quick website, and while he could easily add a few lines of code to his website and enable credit card payments through a payment gateway offered through Square or Stripe, he realizes that he needs to offer more ways to pay.

BUY NOW PAY LATER

Instead of traditional invoicing with "net 30" terms, he looks at "buy now pay later" options offered through companies like Affirm and Klarna. In this model, the buyer can opt to pay later, but the Merchant is paid right away.

For example, a large grocery store places an order for $10,000 and wants to pay in thirty days. On Mufasa's website, instead of entering a credit card, they choose the "Buy Now Pay Later" option. When this happens, the "Buy Now Pay Later" provider sends money to Mufasa's bank account typically the next day and then collects from the grocery store on whatever cadence they requested. For this service, the "Buy Now Pay Later" company typically charges Mufasa a percentage of the transaction, which is typically higher than what Mufasa would pay for credit card processing. However, this fee may be worth it in the interim to help manage Mufasa's cash flow.

PAYMENT SERVICE PROVIDER

The "Buy Now Pay Later" company is considered a Payment Service Provider (PSP). They are able to offer the "Buy Now Pay Later" service in addition to accepting credit and debit cards, and they are also able to offer payments through Mobile Wallets like PayPal, Venmo, and Alipay.

> *Key Term: Payment Service Provider (PSP)*
> *A PSP is an aggregator of payment methods. It allows a website operator to get paid via debit cards, mobile wallets, and financing schemes.*

This was very interesting for Mufasa because through one provider he's able to get all of these payment methods online. He knows that if he ever wants to expand internationally or offer his customers additional ways to pay, his PSP can support all of that and funds settlement can happen through a single source.

An additional benefit to a Payment Service Provider is that under the hood, their payment gateway may connect to multiple Merchant Acquirers, offering Mufasa's business redundancy and also the ability to operate internationally without him having to change anything on his website.

LEARNING ABOUT PAYMENTS BY CREATING WORLD CLASS SUPPORT TEAMS

Song Chin has been working in the world of payments for the last fifteen years, helping lead customer experience for Payment Service Provider, Adyen; Issuer Processor, Marqeta; and, more recently, Facebook.

Song got into payments in 2005 while working as a technical Product Manager for Biopartnering, where he was tasked with figuring out how to accept card-based payments on the Biotech Partnering and Events portal. Figuring out how to set up a way to accept payment in 2005 was challenging because he had to work with very difficult to use software. In 2011, he moved on to work for an Application Programming Interface (API—Basically these are things that enable software developers to integrate into various things quickly) company, Mashery. At the time, Stripe and Braintree were getting a lot of press for building Payments APIs that developers loved, so Song built a basic website and inserted a few lines of code from Stripe, and within minutes, he was able to accept card-based payments on his website. He wished that such technologies existed while he was at Biopartnering.

Later on, he stumbled into his role at Adyen, a Payment Processor, when a recruiter introduced him to a small team of fifteen people in the San Francisco office. In the early days,

Adyen could not only accept card-based payments but also alternative payments like IDeal, Giropay, and Sofort. As their customers started asking for more forms of payment, Ayden began to accept other forms like Alipay and WeChat. Later, they expanded beyond the digital world to accept payments via POS systems as well.

There were no guides at the time of how to do these types of integrations, and through curiosity, the team at Adyen built solutions to these problems. Each of these solutions had issues, and Song learned about these first as he headed up the customer experience team. The customer experience team was the first line of support to Adyen's customers who were large Merchants such as Google, Facebook, and Uber. Any time a Merchant couldn't process a transaction, Song's team would get a call. Through troubleshooting, Song was able to learn the world of Payment Gateways and Acquiring.

A few years later, Song was looking for his next challenge and took an offer at Marqeta, where he led customer experience. In the early days, I was fortunate to have Song as my desk neighbor, and we got a chance to learn about the world of Issuing together, primarily because the product team would launch a product, and he would be the first person to tell us about where things are breaking.

Song learned about payments not by just reading manuals but rather seeing where there were points in the customer experience that were breaking. He also saw how the lives of his customers were so deeply impacted by payments. The world of payments is moving at an even faster pace now that there are companies like Adyen, Stripe, and Marqeta, which are abstracting the complexity of payments and delivering easy to use APIs to developers and entrepreneurs.

KEY TAKEAWAYS

- Merchants can start accepting card-based payments quickly if they go through Payments Facilitators (PayFacs).
- As Merchants grow their transaction volume for card-based payments, they may want to establish an account directly with a Merchant Acquirer.
- Depending on their stage of growth, different pricing strategies for Merchants do exist.
- Payment Service Providers (PSPs) offer Merchants a multitude of ways of getting paid, including traditional card-based payments, digital wallet payments, and also "Buy Now Pay Later" payment options.

UP NEXT...

Let's see what it takes to create our own debit card through an Issuer Processor, Issuing Bank, and Program Manager.

CHAPTER 8

PAYMENTS ECOSYSTEM PART 4: MAKING PAYMENTS

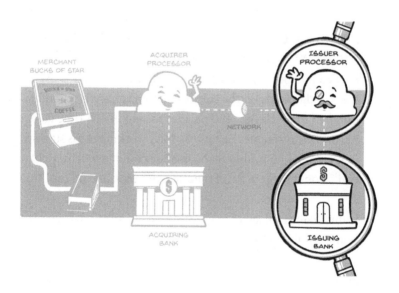

RECAP

In Payments Ecosystem Part 3, we learned:

- Merchants can start accepting or "taking" card-based payments through Merchant Acquirers, Payment Facilitators (PayFacs), and Payment Service Providers (PSPs).
- Merchants pay an Interchange fee to the banks Issuing debit and credit cards.

HOW WOULD ONE GO ABOUT CREATING AND ISSUING THEIR OWN DEBIT OR CREDIT CARD?

Emmet had been watching his dad's donut business grow by leaps and bounds on the sidelines. Donuts have been on his mind all day—classic crullers, glazed, and his all-time favorite, the Boston creme. He's just so busy working at his startup in Oakland and wishes that someone could just drive to his dad's donut shop in San Francisco and pick one up for him.

Immediately, a flash of inspiration hits him! What if he can build a donut delivery business? He will call it DonutDash!

He does a quick search, and there are plenty of people out there who would love to get paid as a driver to pick up and deliver donuts. He also knows that plenty of people are just like him and would love a donut but don't have the time to go out and get it. From his dad's experience, he knows how to accept payments on a website or mobile app by using a Payments Facilitator. But how will he pay the individual donut shops?

Does the driver pay with his own credit card and then submit the receipt to DonutDash to reimburse? Does he carry around a prepaid card from DonutDash with a bunch of money on it that he could potentially go and use for other things like a soda for himself or something even larger like a TV at Best Buy?

Considering that these are contractors, can Emmet trust these drivers to only go and pick up the donuts? The margins on the donut delivery are so razor-thin, even if the driver added a soda to the order, Emmet would be underwater.

DONUTDASH GETS ITS OWN DEBIT CARD

Emmet knew that his new business, DonutDash, would need to issue its own debit card through an Issuer Processor and Program Manager around the block from him in Oakland, Marqeta. He knew that he would need very finite controls on the spend on this debit card. To run a successful donut delivery operation, Emmet would need:

- The ability to link the original order from the DonutDash customer to the actual spend that happens at the restaurant by the driver.
- The ability of the driver to do as many pickups as possible without having to worry about carrying receipts and submitting for reimbursement.

- Prevent fraudulent charges from drivers by controlling the amount that can be spent and when the card can be used.

The solution was a custom DonutDash Mastercard debit card that would be given to each one of its drivers when they started working with DonutDash. But to do that, how can a company whose focus is in delivering donuts for the masses going to build a payments product?

In this chapter, we'll learn about all of the parties involved in Issuing a debit card and the types of responsibilities that each party has.

CARD PROGRAM CONSTRUCT

In this case, DonutDash would not have an issue distributing these cards. They would have plenty of drivers who could use the card to simplify their donut delivery process. In this example, we will start with DonutDash as the Co-Brand Partner. You can think of them much like when Delta airlines issues an American Express card.

- DonutDash Driver is the cardholder
- DonutDash is the Co-Brand Partner
- Mastercard is the Card Network
- Moneybin Bank is the Issuing Bank
- Marqeta is the Program Manager
- Marqeta is the Issuer/Processor

Key Term: Co-Brand Partner
This is typically a brand or company that is marketing the card. This is the brand shown on the card in addition to the card network brand. In some cases, this brand will appear on the front of the card without the Issuing Bank, and in other cases, it may appear on the front with the Issuing Bank.

CARD NETWORK: MASTERCARD

To understand this better, we will start with the Card Network, Mastercard. Mastercard is effectively working to link the Merchant, the local donut shop, to the cardholder, the DonutDash driver. They will route the transactions appropriately, so when the driver swipes his DonutDash Mastercard at Mufasa's Donut Shop, Mastercard will take the information from that swipe at Mufasa's Donut Shop and pass that information to the Issuer Processor, Marqeta, so that an authorization decision can be made. All of this data transmission is done on the Mastercard platform. The card network also facilitates the movement of real money from one bank to another. Essentially, it will take money from DonutDash's Issuing Bank, Moneybin Bank, and move it to Mufasa's Donut Shop's bank to pay for the donut order.

ISSUING BANK: MONEYBIN BANK

The Issuing Bank, Moneybin Bank, takes a license from Mastercard to use its brand on the cards. The cards are technically "Issued by Moneybin Bank." You can think of this as if you have a bank account with Bank of America, your Visa debit card is issued by Bank of America, but since the Bank of

America branding is on the card, Bank of America is also the Co-Brand Partner. In the case of Moneybin Bank, it is serving as just the Issuing Bank. Its role is to ensure that money is being moved appropriately, it is maintaining the connection with its processors and networks. Additionally, Moneybin Bank will provide compliance oversight to all of the programs it issues. For example, it will be the one applying fraud rules to protect cardholders.

PROGRAM MANAGER: MARQETA

> *Key Term: Program Manager*
> *The program manager is the one who is managing the day-to-day operations of the card program including settlement, fraud management, and maintaining the relationship with the Issuing Bank, card manufacturer, card network, and the cardholder.*

The Program Manager is Marqeta. In many cases, the Program Manager is responsible for marketing the cards. However, since DonutDash is the Co-Brand Partner, the marketing aspects go to DonutDash, and it applies some compliance rules that come from Moneybin Bank, the Issuing Bank, to make sure that the cardholders are being communicated with appropriately.

Additionally, the Program Manager is responsible for making sure that settlement is happening appropriately and that fraud is being managed. If cardholders find fraudulent charges and request a chargeback, they will go to the Program Manager to process the chargeback.

The Program Manager also maintains the relationship with the Card Network and the Issuing Bank to ensure that the program is operating correctly. It will also place orders for cards and manage the relationship with the card manufacturer. A bulk of the day-to-day operations falls on the Program Manager.

The Program Manager also ensures that it is doing adequate background checks on its cardholders by performing Know Your Customer (KYC) checks in accordance with the Issuing Bank's requirements.

ISSUER PROCESSOR: MARQETA

The Issuer Processor is the underlying technology that is integrated in with Mastercard, the Card Network. It needs to be able to parse an ISO8583 message (a standard transmission protocol that all Card Networks have agreed on using) from Mastercard in real-time and give a response in less than three seconds. The Issuer Processor licenses a piece of hardware from the Card Network that it keeps in its data centers. This piece of hardware provided by the Card Network is commonly referred to as a Mastercard Interface Processor (MIP) for Mastercard and a VisaNet Integrated Processing (VIP) for Visa. The MIP and the VIP are critical components that an Issuer Processor must have to enable near real-time communication with the Card Networks. The Card Networks typically do not give out too many MIPs or VIPs, which is why the actual number of Issuer Processors is limited.

ISSUER PROCESSOR APPROVES OR DECLINES TRANSACTIONS

When the driver swipes the DonutDash co-branded card at Mufasa's Donut Shop, the Issuer Processor, Marqeta, will receive an amount and location of the swipe and then it will make a decision to approve (authorize) or decline the transaction. It can do this by looking at various spending limits, the balance on the card, and any Merchant category-based restrictions. If everything looks good, the Issuer Processor, Marqeta, can send a message to Mastercard, the Card Network, to approve the transaction.

ISSUER PROCESSOR ENABLES WAYS FOR CO-BRAND PARTNERS TO INTEGRATE WITH IT

Additionally, the role of the Issuer Processor is to provide ways for the Co-Brand Partner to integrate with it. So, for example, when swipes occur, the Co-Brand Partner, Donut-Dash, may want to be alerted in real-time of the swipe, the amount, location, and maybe some other bits of information. Alternatively, the Co-Brand Partner, DonutDash, may want the ability to turn on and off cards through their app or even order cards from their own app. The Issuer Processor, Marqeta, will provide this via Application Program Interfaces (APIs). The Co-Brand Partner, DonutDash, would get documentation from the Issuer Processor, Marqeta, on how to integrate in with its APIs and bake these features into their applications.

MARQETA: JIT FUNDING

Marqeta's modern issuing platform is capable of offering its Co-Brand Partners like DonutDash the ability to authorize their own transactions, which is exactly what Emmet needed to prevent card fraud from its drivers. This technology can send the details from the card swipe to DonutDash in near real-time and request that DonutDash approve or decline the transaction. This is referred to as Just-in-Time (JIT) funding, where the DonutDash cards will always have $0 balance on them. Based on certain business rules such as geolocation of the driver and the donut price, DonutDash would:

1. Send an approval message to Marqeta.
2. At that very instant, Marqeta will fund the transaction for the exact amount of the swipe.
3. The transaction will be approved.
4. The swipe will take that exact money off, leaving the driver with a $0 debit card balance at the end of the transaction.
5. All of this happens in less than three seconds.
6. The DonutDash driver would get a receipt and he is off with his delivery.

If for example, a DonutDash driver was to swipe for an amount that is greater than the expected amount of the swipe, that is, he added a bottled water for himself to the order, DonutDash could decline the transaction. Alternatively, if the DonutDash driver is at a location that he should not be at and tries to spend using the card, DonutDash can also decline the transaction.

ISSUER PROCESSOR PROVIDES REPORTING TO THE ISSUING BANK

The Issuer Processor, Marqeta, is also responsible for providing reporting to Moneybin Bank, the Issuing Bank, for all of the swipes that occurred in a day, and when funds are loaded and unloaded from cards. It will also tell Moneybin Bank, the Issuing Bank, who the users of these cards are.

Settlement data from Mastercard, the Card Network, will be sent to Marqeta, the Program Manager, so that settlement can happen via Marqeta, the Issuer Processor.

CO-BRAND PARTNER: DONUTDASH

The card will be branded with the DonutDash logo and DonutDash is responsible for marketing the card. Considering that this is a business card, the distribution of the cards is made simple because they are distributing the cards to all drivers who contract for them. However, for a card that goes to consumers, like the Delta SkyMiles card, Delta is responsible for marketing this card through its existing user base, billboards, magazine ads, online ads, and so on.

ECONOMICS

One of the key benefits of creating a card is that the card Issuer enjoys revenue coming in the form of Interchange. The Merchant, Dad's Donut Shop, essentially is paying three fees to accept payment from a debit or credit card. Mufasa, the Merchant, agrees to this because he knows that he can increase his sales by accepting cards. At the time of the card swipe, Mufasa's Donut Shop will pay these fees:

ACQUIRER FEE

Usually, a flat fee that is paid per transaction to the Merchant Acquirer, Payments Facilitator, or Payment Gateway. This is essentially the supplier of the card terminal or online payment gateway.

NETWORK ASSESSMENT FEE

This is a small percentage of the transaction value that is sent directly to the Card Network to manage the flow of data transmission. So, this fee would go to Mastercard.

INTERCHANGE

This is a small percentage of the transaction that is sent to the Issuer of the card. We will discuss how it is split amongst the Co-Brand Partner, Program Manager, Issuing Bank, and Issuer Processor.

HOW DOES THE NETWORK MAKE MONEY?

Mastercard gets paid in multiple ways. It collects the Network Assessment from the Merchant at the time of swipe. Additionally, it will charge the Issuer for reporting fees and other licensing fees. Because the Card Network is in the middle, it is able to extract revenue from both the Acquiring and Issuing sides, but the amounts per transaction are rather low because they want to encourage higher transaction volumes. The Card Network doesn't directly touch the Interchange, it is simply passed from the Merchant to the Card Issuer.

HOW DOES THE PROGRAM MANAGER MAKE MONEY?

The Program Manager is typically managing the day-to-day operations of the program and thus takes the bulk of the Interchange. Depending on the arrangements it has with its Issuing Bank and Issuer Processor, the Program Manager may decide to give a certain portion of the Interchange to the Co-Brand Partner.

The Program Manager could also provide the end card-holder with "cash back," which in most cases is limited to certain categories.

HOW DOES THE ISSUING BANK MAKE MONEY?

The Issuing Bank will have an arrangement with the Program Manager in most cases. It may charge the Program Manager fees for setting up bank accounts, performing compliance audits, and general oversight. This could be flat monthly fees, transaction-based fees, or a percentage of the Interchange revenue earned.

The Issuing Bank is also sponsoring the Bank Identification Number (BIN, which represents the first six digits on the card) that the DonutDash Mastercard goes under. Mastercard will license this number to the Issuing Bank, and thus will charge the bank for this license. Note, Mastercard will not provide a license to a non-bank entity, and thus, every card program requires an Issuing Bank. The Issuing Bank has the option to just pass this cost on to the Program Manager or even add a markup on these items.

Furthermore, the Issuing Bank gets deposits from the Co-Brand Partner for use in spend transactions and may choose to earn interest on these deposits.

HOW DOES THE ISSUER PROCESSOR MAKE MONEY?

The Issuer Processor typically makes money as a utility. It will charge money based on the number of cards shipped out or the number of accounts it needs to maintain in its system. It may also make money on each transaction. There may be arrangements in which it participates in a percentage of the Interchange earning that the Program Manager is making.

In the example we are using, where DonutDash is the Co-Brand partner, Marqeta is the Issuer Processor and Program Manager, Marqeta will typically provide a portion of the Interchange revenue to the Co-Brand Partner and also pay fees to the Issuing Bank, Moneybin Bank, for sponsoring the program. In the industry, this is typically referred to as revenue share or Interchange share.

HOW DOES THE CO-BRAND PARTNER MAKE MONEY?

The Co-Brand Partner may have an arrangement with the Program Manager to get a cut of the Interchange Revenue. In most cases, this is on a sliding scale, so as transaction volume grows, the percentage of the Interchange Revenue increases. This revenue share could go into offsetting the cost of card production and also aid in paying for chargebacks or fraud.

In the case where the Co-Brand Partner is offering a credit card, it could take on the burden of calculating interest, underwriting, and collections. This could be done by the Co-Brand Partner or sent to a credit card servicer to manage. Revenue for the Co-Brand Partner can be made on interest charged to credit card holders for nonpayment or if they need to delay payment.

FOUNDER STORY: JASON GARDNER OF MARQETA

Back in 2010, Jason Gardner and his friend, Sukhi Singh, were sitting at a small sushi restaurant in the Mission District in San Francisco having dinner. Jason pulled out his wallet to pay and found out that he had a number of coupons, gift cards, and Groupons. It dawned on him that these mechanisms actually created more friction in payments than it did good. He wondered, *Wouldn't it be great if I could keep all of my discounts, Groupons, and coupons all on one card that can be used anywhere?*

Upon digging into this further, at the register, he found that the main cash register was surrounded by all sorts of other gadgets, iPads, Android Tablets, custom devices for different loyalty programs, and then finally, the main terminal that is used to pay, the credit card terminal.

Most of the time, the person at the register didn't even know how to use all of these devices to complete the transaction. He also thought, *Geez, this must be a nightmare to reconcile for the restaurant owner.* So, he decided to really dig into this. He found that this is a pretty common problem, for most consumers and also restaurant owners preferred to be paid via credit card or via cash, the other mechanisms for payment became really cumbersome.

He found that the major credit card networks, Visa, Mastercard, Discover, and American Express have already figured out a pretty nice system. The restaurant owner buys a card terminal or credit card machine from a Merchant Acquirer or Payments Facilitator, and the end customer gets a card, be it a debit card or credit card from their bank.

Having sold his last company, Property Bridge, which was also a Payments Company specializing in helping landlords collect from their tenants, he had some insights already into how payments generally worked and he started reaching out to the networks to try to understand how these cards worked.

He found that replacing the cash register at the restaurant is going to be a big challenge, and he was intrigued by what actually was already there—the card terminal. Now the question became, how can he get a card that is smart enough to know that he has a prepaid offer at a sushi restaurant AND also at his favorite ice cream shop and that those prepaid offers should be able to maintain distinct balances? That is, his prepaid offer at the sushi restaurant was $50 and at the ice cream shop, it was $20. How could he do it with a single piece of plastic?

That single piece of plastic carries a ton of information on its black magnetic stripe on the back. But how does the data get transferred on to the black magnetic stripe? How does the restaurant know that Jason even has a balance on that card or he has credit available from his bank to be able to pay for this?

He found that this world of payments was needlessly complicated. After digging into this, he found that getting a card program up and running could take months, if not close to a year. There weren't many good developer tools that could help him build this, and in general, it was hard to gain an understanding of how all of this works.

Jason knew he needed to solve this and that's why he decided to build an Issuer Processor from the ground up to allow for these multiple Groupon-like prepaid offers to show up on a single card. This later became the basis for Marqeta.

KEY TAKEAWAYS
- Businesses can create their own debit or credit cards as a Co-Brand Partner.
- Cards are issued through Issuing Banks.
- Co-Brand Partners can earn Interchange revenue from a Merchant every time their card is swiped.
- The Issuer Processor approves or declines transactions and can also provide APIs for Co-Brand Partners to leverage in their applications.

UP NEXT...
We will explore why it is important to "Know Your Customer."

PART 3

DIGGING DEEPER

CHAPTER 9

DIGGING DEEPER PART 1: KYC

WHY IS CONFIRMING THE IDENTITY OF A USER REQUIRED IN THE PAYMENTS SPACE?

Key Term: Know Your Customer (KYC)
KYC or Know Your Customer is a practice in the banking and financing industry used to attach some form of identity to the user of a product.

In the case of cards and bank accounts, a user needs to prove that they are who they say they are. In most cases in the US, a user can prove who they are by providing their social security number, date of birth, and full legal name. With that combination, KYC providers such as Ideology, Identity Mind, Block Score, Experian, Lexis/Nexis, and Persona could go out and find more information about you to prove you are who you say you are. Usually, these services search for public records like tax returns or even do a mild credit check to determine that you are a real person.

These providers will also check to make sure that you have not been flagged for any financial crimes or fraud.

WHAT TYPES OF THINGS REQUIRE KYC?

A prime example of the need for KYC comes when you open up a bank account. Historically, you would go into a bank branch and bring some forms of identity with you to open up a checking account. These could be your social security card, driver's license, some utility bills, and so on. However, with more and more banks going online-only, these artifacts need to be submitted online, presenting challenges in verifying who you are.

In the case of an online bank application at one of these newer "Neo-banks" such as Varo, Chime, MoneyLion, Simple, Branch, or N26, the KYC process typically works like this:

- Create an account in the mobile app by supplying your first name and last name
- Supply your social security number
- Supply your date of birth
- Supply your physical address

Additionally, the KYC providers may also ask for other things like:

- Phone number
- Email address
- Previous addresses
- Security questions that only you would know, these are things like previous addresses you have lived at, make

and model of your car, previous year tax return amount, and so on.

- A picture of a driver's license or government ID
- A picture of your passport (primarily if you are new to the US)
- A picture of yourself to match against a passport or driver's license

DO PREPAID CARDS AND GIFT CARDS NEED KYC?

We just discussed banks requiring KYC, and similarly, debit and prepaid card programs also require KYC. But what about those prepaid Visa gift cards I can get at the grocery store? Or the Mastercard gift card I received from Comcast for referring a friend?

This is a unique case. This is because these prepaid gift cards typically can only be loaded up with money once. Once the funds are depleted, then the card becomes useless. Some of these cards allow you to reload funds to them, and to do this, the user must perform KYC before any additional funds are allowed on the prepaid card. The important thing here is that the loading is what invokes the KYC, not the spending. This is because it is possible for bad actors to use these cards for money laundering if KYC was not required.

BRINGING IN MORE CUSTOMERS WHILE KEEPING THE BADDIES OUT

The banks want people to pass through KYC so they can get a customer, but they want to make sure that bad actors are not let into the financial system. However, there may be instances where someone doesn't have much of a financial footprint. This is typical of people coming to the US from other parts of the world. In many cases, it takes them time to get a social security number and to establish themselves in the financial system. This is why it is important to be able to offer other forms of identity verification much like checking government-issued IDs or passports. If the person doesn't have this, then it is increasingly difficult to get into the financial system. These people with a "thin file" are often considered the "unbanked."

FOUNDER STORY: RICK SONG: IDENTITY AS A WAY OF UNDERWRITING WITH PERSONA

Rick Song graduated from Rice University in Texas with a degree in Computer Science in 2013 and decided to take a full-time job working with a small team of engineers at Square Capital. At Square Capital, the primary challenge that they were trying to solve was, how do we get these small Merchants up and running quickly and be able to provide them with loans with a few clicks in the Square Merchant application?

UNDERWRITING BY LOOKING AT SWIPES

Traditionally, getting small business loans was a long process requiring a ton of paperwork and working with slow-moving banks. One point of data that Square had that most traditional banks didn't have is a transaction history of the small business. All card swipes from customers paying this small business were recorded by Square, and Square had a very good sense of the small Merchant's cash flow.

IDENTIFYING THE MOM AND POP SHOPS BY IDENTIFYING "MOM" AND "POP"

However, the more challenging thing was that these Merchants may have been one- or two-person enterprises, and while they may be registered as a legal entity, there wasn't enough data about that legal entity. However, there would be plenty of information about the actual person behind the business. It was enough to perform some basic checks to at least make sure that this person was legitimate, which could be used to help underwrite a loan for their business.

Rick and his team started looking into performing KYC checks on these small business owners. They started evaluating KYC providers, and they found that each provider had its strengths and weaknesses.

When the loan product was first rolled out, users would get stuck in the KYC process. The users were not able to be accurately "identified," and, thus, would end up in a state where they weren't able to "qualify" for a loan even though they had plenty of transaction history. These small business owners were frustrated that they were being turned down for a loan they knew they were "good for," but they just were not able to pass KYC.

HELPING GOOD "MOMS" AND "POPS" GET UNSTUCK

To combat this, Rick's team started stitching together multiple KYC providers, so basically, if their first KYC attempt failed, then it would give the user the ability to try to verify another way. Sometimes, it would require the small business owner to provide some other piece of information to prove their identity, and this dramatically increased the number of people able to take out a loan via Square Capital.

ASK ONLY FOR DOCUMENTATION RELEVANT TO "MOM" AND "POP"

Rick's key learning was, don't leave a user hanging; if they fail the first time, give them a few different options or tries to pass. Furthermore, it is better to step up the authentication progressively, instead of asking for everything upfront. Imagine a form that looks like this:

- First Name
- Last Name
- Home Address
- Email Address
- Phone Number
- Social Security Number
- Passport Number
- Driver's License Number
- Date of Birth
- Previous three addresses

Instead of asking all users for all of these things, he opted to only ask for things as needed for that user, trying to verify a person every step of the way. This made the form less daunting for users and it also allowed the forms to become dynamic for each type of person.

BUT WHAT ABOUT THOSE PEOPLE WHO ARE UNBANKED/UNDER-BANKED AND IMMIGRANTS?

Square was keen on being able to empower ANYONE to become a small business owner, and it would have been hypocritical if Square only offered those who are already well banked to get "even more banked." So, in addition to being able to operate internationally, Square had to come up with solutions to allow people with very little documented history in the US, namely immigrants, to be able to conduct business and get the same level of banking/financing that Square offers to everyone else.

Rick got the insight that in reality, everyone still has something about them documented somewhere. It might not be a document from the US, but they will have some form of a document. As long as the user is guided to providing that document that proves their identity, there will be an identity service that will be able to find them and be able to prove that this person is who they say they are. At Square, Rick's team had to integrate with more than twenty services to really enable this (PayPal has integrated with over 140 services).

BUILDING A DEVELOPER FRIENDLY IDENTITY PLATFORM

As Rick was building this identity platform for Square, he did a lot of vendor evaluations and realized how difficult and cumbersome it was for a business to get set up with KYC providers. None of these KYC providers were able to provide him with a quick demo that he, as an engineer, could try out on his own before deciding to buy it. Furthermore, he realized how complicated it was to integrate with all of these different services and wanted to provide a developer-friendly set of tools to build out KYC flows that will help identify and bring in as many users to that developer's platform as possible.

In 2018, Rick's roommate and former internship classmate from Kleiner Perkins, an engineer from Dropbox, was looking to do something new, preferably in collaboration with Rick. Rick, a self-professed non-entrepreneur, thought about all of the things that he enjoyed doing in his spare time and realized that he was obsessed with the KYC space and the ability to identify users. So, while he never initially planned to start a company, he knew that he could spend his entire life working on this problem of identity.

So, a few weeks later, he spoke with his managers at Square about this concept and they encouraged him to go ahead and start a company on the subject of identity. With this blessing, he realized he needed to become an entrepreneur and henceforth co-founded Persona.

Persona is a KYC platform that does a lot of the KYC legwork to connect to multiple services to identify a person in the background, while still providing a great user experience for the end consumer. His product powers a number of fintech and Payments Companies.

KEY TAKEAWAYS
- Financial products need the ability to verify the identity of the user to prevent bad actors from entering into the financial system.
- Sometimes it can be hard to identify people because they may not have much financial data available about them.

- As banks are going digital-only, there needs to be technology to support identifying people in an easy, digital way.

UP NEXT...

We'll take a look at the differences between a debit card and a credit card.

CHAPTER 10

DIGGING DEEPER PART 2: CREDIT CARDS VERSUS DEBIT CARDS

WHAT'S THE DIFFERENCE BETWEEN A DEBIT CARD AND A CREDIT CARD?

Twenty-three percent of Millennials don't even carry credit cards, according to TD Bank's Annual Consumer Spending Survey.[10]

Debit cards prevent users from spending more than what is currently available in their bank account. This is a fundamental shift in how people spend because people are not likely to spend more than what is in their bank account and, thus, cash flow really makes a difference in how people spend. The spending habits of someone who is living paycheck to paycheck and refuses to use a credit card is vastly different

---

10　"TD Bank's Annual Consumer Spending Index Reveals Credit Knowledge Gap Exists Among Millenials," PR Newswire, accessed on January 26, 2020.

from someone who is living paycheck to paycheck but still opts into using a credit card.

Furthermore, not everyone can qualify for a credit card or may have bad credit preventing them from getting a credit card.

So, why is it that the mainstream media, when talking about payment cards typically say "credit card," when in fact they should say "debit card"? **The fundamental truth is that most people can't tell the difference.**

The only key distinction is that a debit card will have the word "debit" on it, and a credit card will have the word "credit" on it.

At the end of the day, both are pieces of plastic that are used to buy things. They will usually have the network logo of Visa or Mastercard on the front, with perhaps some indication of which bank this card is with. Both will contain:

- A sixteen-digit card number
- An expiration date
- A CVV number on the back of the card
- Your name

Some credit cards offer different network logos, so for higher-end credit cards, you may see the word "Visa Signature," or "Mastercard World" or in the case of Mastercard, the orange and yellow circles are reflected as two silver circles.

Higher-end credit cards may also be made out of aluminum or out of a heavier plastic to give it a more premium feel.

USER INTERACTIONS

However, the way that you interact with a credit card and a debit card is fundamentally different. In the world of credit cards, the cardholder is typically paying the Issuing Bank back on a monthly basis, so essentially, the Issuing Bank is providing a loan to the cardholder for as much as thirty days (can vary depending on your payment cycle). If the loan is not paid off in full by the payment cutoff date, then the balance accrues interest charges. Most people don't like the concept of interest charges because many times this calculation can be confusing, and they also don't want to worry about forgetting to pay their credit card bill.

Authorization and clearing work very similar on both credit cards and debit cards. When a card is swiped at a Merchant, the Merchant is paid by the Issuing Bank on the cardholder's behalf. In debit, these funds come out directly from the cardholder's checking account, while with credit, these funds are deducted from a cardholder's available line of credit. The Issuing Bank is using its funds to pay for the merchandise, and the cardholder is expected to pay back the Issuing Bank. The transaction flows work the same still, instead of checking the cardholder's checking account balance, the Issuer Processor is checking for the cardholder's available credit line with the Issuing Bank.

DOES USING CREDIT VERSUS DEBIT MATTER TO THE MERCHANT?

The distinctions between credit and debit begin to matter more at the Merchant level because the Merchant will pay different Interchange rates depending on the type of card. Typically, Interchange is higher on a credit card versus a debit card. We will discuss this further in the next chapter.

ACCEPTANCE

Another key difference is in acceptance, especially when it comes to hotel stays and car rentals. To the end Merchant, credit cards are actually a more guaranteed form of payment because they know that they will be paid by the Issuing Bank regardless of if the cardholder has enough money in their bank account. Hotels and car rental companies will typically place a funds hold of the total stay amount plus an allocation for incidentals on the card at time of check-in. If the cardholder doesn't have enough money to cover the funds held in their bank account and are using a debit card, then they may not be able to check into their hotel or rent their car.

The travel industry, in general, prefers credit cards and is willing to pay higher Interchange rates for this risk mitigation.

KEY TAKEAWAYS
- Millennials are preferring debit cards over credit cards.
- You can get a credit card if you are deemed as "creditworthy."
- Some industries prefer accepting credit cards because the funds are guaranteed by the Issuing Bank.

- Merchants will pay higher Interchange on credit cards versus debit cards.

UP NEXT...

We'll take an in-depth look into how Interchange is calculated.

CHAPTER 11

DIGGING DEEPER
PART 3: INTERCHANGE

WHAT IS INTERCHANGE AND HOW IS IT CALCULATED?

Key Term: Interchange
Interchange is a fee that is sent from the Merchant to the Issuing Bank of the card being swiped.

If we go back to our original story of Emmet's Mocha from Bucks of Star Coffee, you may recall that Emmet has a Mastercard debit card that is issued by Moneybin Bank. When Emmet buys his mocha from Bucks of Star Coffee, then Bucks of Star Coffee is paying an Interchange fee to Emmet's Issuing Bank, Moneybin Bank. This is calculated based on a fairly complex rate table set by Visa and Mastercard. Interchange, in addition to the Network Assessment and the Acquirer fee, is charged to the Merchant. However, only the Interchange portion of the transaction is sent to the Card Issuer. In most cases, the Acquirer fee is a flat fee per transaction that is charged at the end of the month by the

Merchant Acquirer or the provider of the payment terminal or payment gateway. A small Network Assessment that the Merchant is paying to Mastercard is required, which can be thought of as the toll to use the Mastercard rails.

The two major factors that define the Interchange rate is the type of card and the type of Merchant. Emmet has a "consumer Mastercard debit card" from Moneybin Bank. He is buying his Mocha from Bucks of Star Coffee, which is registered as a Merchant Type of "Fast Food."

TYPE OF MERCHANT

Each Merchant is classified with a Merchant Category Code or MCC. This code is used depending on the products/services they offer and what industry they belong in. Certain industries have a larger quantity of transactions than others while other industries yield higher dollar amounts than others and, thus, the card Networks have come up with pricing procedures to factor this in. Additionally, there are types of Merchants that attract customers that may be considered higher risk, because a higher risk of chargebacks or fraud can exist. These are things that are part of very complex logic that the networks have put together over decades.

TYPE OF CARD

The card networks also have different categories of cards. The three main types of cards are debit, credit, and prepaid. Prepaid and debit are very similar because they are based on a "good funds model" meaning that these cards need real money behind them to work. Credit, on the other hand, relies on another entity that is underwriting the credit for these people.

DEBIT CARDS

The two primary types of debit cards are standard debit cards or prepaid cards. Debit cards also offer two modes, a Credit Mode and a Debit Mode.

DEBIT CARD MODES

The best way to visualize this is to think about a typical payment terminal. When you use your debit card, it will ask you for "Credit" or "Debit" at the terminal. If you select "Credit," it will typically ask you to sign the receipt or sign on the terminal. If you select "Debit," then it will ask you to enter your four-digit PIN. The Credit Mode is also referred to as "Dual-Message," which means that when the card is swiped, it will place a hold for the funds immediately (the first part of Dual-Message) and thus on your online banking screen, you will see the transaction as "Pending." The next day, a clearing transaction will post (the second part of the Dual-Message), and then this will move the transaction from pending to completed. In contrast, when you run in Debit Mode, or as a "Single-Message" transaction, the funds are immediately moved to the completed state. A second clearing transaction does not occur for this.

DUAL-MESSAGE VERSUS SINGLE MESSAGE—WHO CARES?

The mode or the message type matters because of the Interchange charged to the Merchant.

When you take a Visa debit card and run it as a "Credit" transaction, this will be routed along the Visa Dual-Message rails and will, for the sake of simplicity, charge the Merchant around 1 percent to 2 percent of the transaction value for the Interchange. In contrast, if you used the "Debit" mode or Single-Message, this Interchange drops to something typically below 0.5 percent.

For Merchants, this difference can be significant, and while most Merchants offer both, they are getting more clever in routing transactions to reduce the Interchange as much as possible. Walmart has programmed its terminals to route all debit card-based transactions on Debit Mode and not requiring the user to enter a PIN, which is referred to as "PIN-less debit." While this mechanism increases the risk for the Merchant because the consumer didn't enter in this PIN as a confirmation that this is their card, the Merchant could incur a higher-volume chargeback that it won't win. In the case of Walmart, it is fine with this level of risk considering that as a percentage of transactions, the vast majority of the transactions will go through just fine, and this 0.5 percent difference could save the retailer millions.

To most consumers, they aren't able to tell the difference of being automatically routed to the Debit Mode versus Credit Mode, especially if they don't need to enter in their PIN.

CONSUMER VERSUS COMMERCIAL DEBIT CARDS

An additional layer determining Interchange rates for debit cards running on the Credit Mode is if the card is considered a "consumer" card or a "commercial" card. The real difference here lies in where the funds are coming from.

COMMERCIAL DEBIT CARDS—HIGHER INTERCHANGE

A debit card that is funded by a company is being used for expenses and will command a higher Interchange rate (on the higher end of the 1 to 2 percent spectrum). This is the type of card that Emmet is issuing to the drivers for his donut delivery business, DonutDash.

CONSUMER DEBIT CARDS—LOWER INTERCHANGE

A debit card where it is funded by the cardholder via a direct deposit from his or her employer, or via depositing checks, is considered a consumer card and commands a lower Interchange rate (on the lower end of the 1 to 2 percent spectrum). This is the type of card that Emmet used to buy his Mocha. It is a basic debit card issued by his bank, Moneybin Bank.

CREDIT CARDS

Credit cards typically command higher Interchange rates (between 2 to 3 percent of the transaction value) because there are more costs to offering credit to customers for the Issuer, because in essence, the Issuer is offering a thirty-day loan to the buyer and, thus, incurs the cost of capital. Furthermore, Merchants are charged more for this because it is known statistically that those who use credit cards spend more frequently and have a higher capacity to spend. Furthermore, since the funds are backed by the Issuer, the Merchant will have a lower risk of chargeback.

The networks also offer different levels of credit cards like Visa Signature or Mastercard World. These are credit cards only offered to users with a higher credit profile, good examples of this is the Chase Sapphire line of cards (Visa Signature) or the Citi Prestige Card (Mastercard World). These cards typically command the highest Interchange rates. So, for example, a basic Visa credit card would command approximately 2 percent of the transaction value as Interchange, a premium Visa card could command up to 3 percent of the transaction value as Interchange.

OTHER MEANS OF CONTROLLING INTERCHANGE

DURBIN

Considering that most cards are issued by Chase, Citi, Wells Fargo, and Bank of America, and all of these banks have assets greater than $10 billion, they fall into the "regulated" Interchange category as defined by the Durbin Amendment. The Durbin Amendment to the Dodd-Frank rule basically regulates Interchange that can be earned by large Issuers. An Issuer who has $10 billion in assets or more falls into the "regulated" Interchange category. Regulated Issuers get 21 cents plus 0.05 percent of the transaction amount, with another penny for approved fraud controls. This means that the Chase Sapphire Preferred card, which is a Visa Signature credit card, actually receives much lower Interchange than a premium Visa card offered through a bank with assets less than $10 billion. However, because of the volume of cards issued via Chase, it can make up for this in total volume.

CLEARING TIME

Merchants who clear transactions faster can also qualify for better Interchange rates and this is factored into their Interchange rate table.

TRACK 3 DATA

Some Merchants are actually able to provide receipt level detail to the networks. This means that they can actually send to the network and the Issuer the actual items they bought in the purchase. This is referred to as Track 3 data. When Merchants provide this data, then the card networks will allow the Merchant to pay lower Interchange on the transactions where they provided this Track 3 data. For example, if Emmet had bought a mocha and a croissant from Bucks of Star Coffee, the Track 3 data will show both the mocha and the croissant, instead of just showing the total dollar amount of the swipe.

PRIVATE LABEL CARDS

While some large retailers have taken the approach of reducing Interchange costs by forcing all of its debit card customers to transact via the PIN-less Debit method, some retailers have taken a different approach by offering their own private label cards.

Macys, Target, Gap, and many more retailers offer a private label credit card. These cards don't have any network affiliation and can only work at the stores that issue these cards. Since no network affiliation exists, the terminal will speak directly to the Issuing Bank (which may be the same as the Acquiring Bank in this case).

When customers use a private label card, the retailer offering the private label card gains in a few ways:

- It has direct access to the customer's spending data
- It reserves a spot in the customer's wallet, having the retailer's brand top of mind
- No Interchange paid to the Issuer (instant savings of anywhere between 0.5 percent and 3 percent)
- Little or no fees paid to the Acquirer because, most likely, the Acquiring Bank and Issuing Bank are the same
- Brand loyalty

In many cases, the retailer is able to offer cashback to users of its private-label card because it is avoiding the Interchange costs. This is able to create incredible value for its customers who opt into this card.

CO-BRAND CARDS

Best Buy and Amazon, on the other hand, took a different approach. Instead of offering a private label Best Buy card or private label Amazon card, Best Buy partnered with Mastercard and Citi to offer the Best Buy Mastercard, and Amazon partnered with Visa and Chase to offer the Amazon Prime Rewards Visa Card. In this model, these retailers are using the Mastercard and Visa rails to complete the transaction. Just like any other credit card, Best Buy and Amazon are paying Interchange to the Issuer, which is Citi for Best Buy and Chase for Amazon. It is paying a network assessment to Mastercard and Visa. However, since the arrangement is directly with Mastercard and Visa, the networks, and Citi and Chase, the Issuing Banks, it is likely that Best Buy and Amazon are getting rebates from Mastercard and Visa to reduce or potentially wash the network assessment, and also getting rebates from Citi and Chase to reduce or wash the Interchange fees. Best Buy and Amazon then use these rebates to offer rewards points to their customers that can be converted to rewards certificates or cashback. Since this card can also be used as a regular credit card outside of Best Buy and Amazon, Citi and Chase can make revenue by earning Interchange on transactions outside of Best Buy and Amazon. This is why sometimes you will receive emails from Citi or Chase to spend outside of Best Buy and Amazon to earn extra rewards. These retailers and Issuing Banks want this to be your primary credit card, earn rewards for any kind of spend, and redeem these rewards at that retailer, thus bringing you back into Best Buy or Amazon to purchase more from them.

KEY TAKEAWAYS

- Interchange is a fee that the Merchant pays to the Card Issuer.
- Merchant type, card type, and a number of other factors determine how much Interchange the Issuer will receive per transaction.
- Credit cards command higher Interchange than debit cards.

- Debit card modes can also change the amount a Merchant pays in Interchange.
- Merchants create private label cards or co-brand cards to help reduce Interchange costs.

UP NEXT...

How to leverage other technologies like ACH, Zelle, Peer-to-Peer, Wire Transfers, and RTP to move money.

CHAPTER 12

DIGGING DEEPER PART 4: MOVING MONEY WITHOUT THE CARD NETWORKS

WHAT ARE THE ALTERNATIVES FOR MOVING MONEY BESIDES THE CARD NETWORKS?

Moving money via cards is fast, efficient, and widely accepted. However, there are alternative ways to move money that in many ways are less expensive than card-based transfers. Here are the technologies we will be exploring:

- ACH
- Direct Deposit
- Peer-to-Peer
- Zelle
- Wire Transfers
- Real-Time Payments (RTP)

ACH

Over 82 percent of all electronic payments in the US are run today via Automated Clearing House (ACH) according to Plaid.[11] These traditionally are bank-to-bank transfers and require users to supply their bank account and routing numbers. Typically, if you are paying for your utilities via their website, you would enter your bank account number and routing number (found at the bottom of a check). Or when you receive your paycheck and want to enroll in direct deposit, this is also a form of ACH, where you supply your employer with your bank account and routing number so they can deposit your payroll check electronically.

> *Key Term: ACH*
> *ACH or Automated Clearing House is a technology that is offered by the "Clearing House," which is a nonprofit organization. It is a network of banks that have come together to enable the movement of money interbank through the use of bank account and routing numbers. This is a batch process.*

ACH is fairly efficient and relatively inexpensive in comparison to card-based transactions. In bulk, it makes sense to submit and receive payments via this method strictly from a cost perspective. However, it isn't the fastest mode of moving money. ACH is a batch process with defined "cutoff windows." If you don't post an ACH transaction

---

11 "A modern guide to ACH: Everything you need to know to start accepting ACH payments," Plaid, accessed on January 26, 2020.

before the cutoff window (specific time defined by your bank), then the transaction will not be processed until the next cutoff time.

If you are looking to send and receive money via ACH, you need to work with a bank that can serve as the ACH Originator or Originating Debit Financial Institution (ODFI). You will create a file with debits and credits; formatted in a NACHA format (a format that was defined by the National Automated Clearing House Association).

A good way to understand the flow of ACH payments is to examine how it is actually used in practice. Emmet has set up auto-pay with his electric company, PG&E.

Here is what Emmet needs to do to set up ACH payments with PG&E:

1. Emmet logs into PG&E's website.
2. Emmet enrolls in auto-pay, which will pull funds from his bank account on the fifteenth of every month (if the fifteenth falls on a weekend, funds will be pulled on the Friday prior to the fifteenth).
3. Emmet adds his checking account and routing number from his bank, Moneybin Bank.
4. He consents to allow his electric company, PG&E, to perform an ACH Pull from his bank account.

After setup, Emmet receives his first invoice:

1. Emmet receives his bill on the first of the month for $53.97.

2. On the thirteenth or fourteenth of the month, PG&E, through their bank, sends a NACHA file to the Federal Reserve Bank (the Fed).
3. The Fed then takes that NACHA file and parses out only the transactions that will be going to Moneybin Bank.
4. The Fed then sends the NACHA file to Emmet's Bank, Moneybin Bank, requesting $53.97 to be debited from Emmet's account on the fifteenth.
5. Emmet usually maintains at least $1,000 in his bank account at all times.
6. On the fifteenth, Emmet will see a debit of $53.97 from PG&E on his bank statement.
7. PG&E will see a credit in their bank account for $53.97.
8. PG&E will pay an ACH fee to its bank toward the end of the month for all ACHs they "Originated." This is not netted out of the transaction much like card-based transactions.

Emmet receives his second invoice the following month, but he's unable to pay:

1. Emmet receives his bill on the first of the following month for $73.05.
2. On the thirteenth or fourteenth of the month, PG&E, through their bank, sends a NACHA file to the Fed.
3. The Fed then takes that NACHA file and parses out only the transactions that will be going to Moneybin Bank.
4. The Fed then sends the NACHA file to Emmet's Bank, Moneybin Bank, requesting $73.05 to be debited from Emmet's account on the fifteenth.
5. Emmet made a large purchase on the thirteenth and now has only $47.93 in his bank account.

6. On the fifteenth, Emmet will see a debit of $73.05 from PG&E on his bank statement, but now his bank balance has gone negative.

7. PG&E will see a credit in their bank account for $73.05.

8. On the sixteenth, Emmet will receive a $35 overdraft charge from his bank, Moneybin Bank.

9. Moneybin Bank will then process an ACH return to PG&E of $73.05. Note: Moneybin Bank has up to three business days from the effective date of the original ACH Debit transaction to process a return, or the return may be rejected by PG&E's bank.

10. Moneybin Bank will send a NACHA file to the Fed.

11. Moneybin Bank will credit Emmet the $73.05 back to his account, bringing him back positive, but he still will have the $35 overdraft charge from his bank.

12. The Fed will then send the return NACHA file to PG&E's bank.

13. PG&E will see a debit on their bank account for $73.05.

14. PG&E will then send Emmet an email informing him that his payment was returned.

15. Emmet then calls PG&E and pays on the phone with his credit card so his power won't be shut off.

16. Emmet then calls his bank and apologizes profusely for letting his bank account go negative. His bank then waives the $35 overdraft fee "just this once."

17. PG&E will pay an ACH fee to its bank toward the end of the month for all ACH's they "Originated."

18. PG&E will also pay for the ACH return.

19. PG&E will pay the Interchange fee to Emmet's bank, and also pay the network assessment fee to the card network, and the Acquirer fee to its Merchant Acquirer, since it

ended up getting payment from Emmet's credit card over the phone.

This is a bit different from card-based payments because in most cases, a card-based swipe will return a decline message in real-time if the user does not have enough money to cover the charge. ACH has the ability to overdraft someone, whereas cards in most cases will just decline and not cause an overdraft if the cardholder has insufficient funds.

DIRECT DEPOSIT

Key Term: Direct Deposit
A direct deposit is a type of ACH transfer that typically comes from an employer into an employee's bank account.

Once an employee provides their employer with their account and routing number to have their pay directly deposited, the employer no longer needs to send out paper checks to that employee. Paper checks on average cost the employer $4, which includes the cost of printing, mailing, and servicing. In many cases, an employee who opts to receive their money via direct deposit can actually get their money faster because they don't need to wait for their check to be cleared by their bank, which could take several days.

For this reason, employers are pushing employees to set up a direct deposit on the first day they join so they can avoid the cost of mailing the physical check.

When an employer runs payroll, which could be a few days prior to payday, they submit a NACHA file to their bank to initiate an ACH transfer to their employees. The employer's bank then sends this file to the Fed as the ODFI, and the Fed breaks up this file and then sends these files to the banks of the employees so that they can credit the employee's bank accounts. In most cases, this will create an ACH Credit in the employee's bank account.

Historically, it would take three days for ACH to process; however, with faster ACH being offered by most banks, this could post within a day. For this reason, the employer will have in the NACHA file the actual date of the transfer and the date in which they want the funds to be "effective" and available in their employee's bank account.

For example, if the NACHA file is submitted on Wednesday and the employee's bank receives this file on Wednesday, theoretically they can post these funds on the same day. However, if there is an effective date of Friday, then the Fed will not move the funds until Friday.

This is a nuance that neo-banks such as Chime, Varo, and Branch are taking advantage of. Since funds coming from an employer are fairly reliable, versus an ACH from an individual, these neo-banks are comfortable in offering these funds to these employees on the day they receive the NACHA file, so in this case, on Wednesday versus Friday. This becomes an added benefit to banking with these neo-banks versus a traditional bank like Wells Fargo because these neo-banks make these funds available sooner. Essentially, these neo-banks are floating those funds for two days for the employee while waiting for the actual funds to arrive on Friday.

FUTURE OF ACH

NACHA is pushing for faster payments by offering Same-Day ACH. With Same-Day ACH, NACHA files must be received in the morning, and funds can be deposited by the end of the business day (exact timing to be determined by your bank). If this morning cutoff time is missed, then funds will be made available the next business day. Same-Day ACH transactions are restricted to transactions less than $25,000. The ACH process historically would take one-to-three business days for the funds to be moved. Now, funds are moved in the same day.

PEER-TO-PEER AND ACH

A good example of how companies leverage ACH to move money from one person to another is Venmo. Venmo allows users to send each other money instantly.

Handy Randy is a handyman who is working on building a fence for Emmet. He requests half of the money down when he starts the project, and then half when he completes the job. He also goes to Home Depot to pick up supplies for Emmet's fence and then requests reimbursement via Venmo.

For the initial payment, Emmet sent Randy some money via Venmo. However, Emmet didn't have that much money in his Venmo account. He was still able to send the money to Handy Randy instantly through his connected Moneybin

Bank account. Venmo was able to confirm that Emmet was good for the money because Emmet connected his Moneybin Bank account to his Venmo account via Plaid. Venmo then initiates an ACH Debit to Emmet's Moneybin Bank.

This transfer of funds from Emmet's Moneybin Bank to Venmo takes one to two business days via ACH.

However, Handy Randy needs the money now and uses his Venmo card to pay for things right away. Venmo is actually floating money for a few days before it receives Emmet's money from Moneybin Bank.

Similarly, if Handy Randy is ready to transfer some of this money over to his checking account, it may take up to three business days for the money to post. Venmo makes these funds immediately unavailable in the Venmo app while this transfer is happening.

ZELLE

In 2011, JP Morgan Chase, Wells Fargo, and Bank of America got together to find a way to move money from one bank to the next simply and easily. They built a product called clearXchange that later became Zelle. The technology allows movement of money between accounts at different banks much like users would move money within the same bank, much like a ledger transfer. So, for example, if Emmet and Handy Randy were to both bank at Moneybin Bank, and Handy Randy needed $50, Emmet could transfer this money instantly by doing a debit of $50 from his account and then Moneybin Bank would do a credit to Handy Randy's account for $50. This would happen instantaneously and would not require "settlement." This transaction is irrevocable because now the funds are in Handy Randy's account. If Emmet needed that money back, he would need to ask Handy Randy to initiate a transfer from Handy Randy's account for the $50 and this would be treated as a separate and unique transaction.

The banks took this technology and made it so that all of the banks on the Zelle network could use it. In essence, it is a ledger change.

So now, if Emmet's account is at Moneybin Bank, and Handy Randy's account is at Wells Fargo, how would Emmet know how to send money to Handy Randy? For this to work, both Emmet and Handy Randy would need to sign up for the Zelle service through their respective banks by providing their phone number and email address. This way, all Emmet needs to know is Handy Randy's phone number or email address to send money. He doesn't need to know Handy Randy's bank account and routing numbers or even know where Handy Randy banks.

WIRE TRANSFERS

Key Term: Wire Transfer
Wire transfer is a way to move money (usually large dollar amounts) from one bank to another securely and quickly by using the account and routing numbers of the sending and receiving banks. This is typically done much faster than ACH.

When making a large purchase such as a home, one of the most secure ways to send money quickly is via Wire Transfer. In the US, Fedwire, through the Federal Reserve is the primary means to wire funds from one bank to another and is supported by just about every bank in the US. Additionally, The Clearing House also provides a wire service called Clearing House Interbank Payments System (CHIPS).

When Emmet was buying a house, he needed to wire his deposit to the title company that is holding the funds until the house closes with the seller, Paul. Emmet initiated a wire transfer through his Moneybin Bank web application.

When he did this, he got a call from Moneybin Bank in about one hour to confirm the wire transfer. When he confirmed and paid the $25 wire fee, the money was pushed out of his bank account and into the bank account of the title company. Emmet then needed to call the title company to confirm that the money arrived. The title company checked their account and saw the money came in via wire. At that point, Emmet was able to move to the next step in his home buying experience.

The technology is very simple in that there is no settlement much like Zelle. The money moves instantly; however, humans are involved to confirm the money has moved, and thus there was about an hour delay.

REAL-TIME PAYMENTS (RTP)

While wire transfers are primarily used for large transfers, the technology can be used for smaller payments. The costs of wire are high because of the humans involved to confirm the money movement. This could be reduced if there weren't humans involved. However, would people be comfortable moving large sums of money without this type of confirmation? Most likely not, but perhaps for smaller dollar amounts, it may make sense.

Key Term: Real-Time Payments (RTP)
RTP is a way to push money within seconds
by sending money directly to a bank account
offered by The Clearing House.

In 2017, The Clearing House announced the availability of the Real-Time Payments (RTP) protocol. RTP is a push only transaction and can only work when the sender initiates a push payment. However, the cost needed to be significantly cheaper than the $25 that Emmet paid for his wire transfer when buying his home. After all, paying $25 for even a $100 transfer just wouldn't make sense. So, the cost of RTP is capped for the banks to $0.045 per transfer, to open up wider spread adoption. This is the end cost for the banks, but the banks are allowed to add a markup to this for their servicing.

This RTP technology becomes very interesting once it becomes more ubiquitous with all banks in that it can compete with Push-to-Card technologies like Visa Direct and Mastercard Send. It is just as fast and cheaper in most cases. The only major drawback to RTP over Push-to-Card is that it doesn't provide an immediate confirmation that the transaction went through.

KEY TAKEAWAYS

- Banks are able to move money via a number of methods in addition to card-based payments.
- ACH accounts for 82 percent of all electronic payments in the US and is relatively inexpensive.
- ACH is getting faster with same-day ACH but still remains batch-based.
- Wire transfers are instant but expensive and used primarily for larger dollar amounts.
- RTP operates like a wire for smaller dollar amounts.
- Money can move from one bank to another through Zelle, which is a way to move money instantly between bank accounts.
- Peer-to-Peer technology offered through companies like Venmo moves money from one person to another primarily through ACH but makes it look instant.

UP NEXT...

We'll learn how to use the Push-to-Card technology to send money to a debit card in seconds.

PART 4

PAYMENTS IN ACTION

CHAPTER 13

PAYMENTS IN ACTION PART 1: PUSH-TO-CARD

IF I AM IN A PINCH, WHAT IS THE FASTEST WAY TO GET MONEY TO MY DEBIT CARD?

"It is six o'clock in the morning and my car broke down. I had $25 to my name and about $5 in my bank account. I get paid every two weeks. I downloaded the Branch app, connected my bank account and debit card, and boom, I got funded $150 in my account. I was able to drop off my car at the shop and take an Uber to get to work on time." explained Khaleel, a manager at a discount retailer.

Branch was able to save Khaleel, our hero from Chapter 1 through Visa Direct and Mastercard Send, two leading providers of Push-to-Card technology. This technology is reliable, and most importantly, fast. In comparison, traditional ACH takes two to three business days, if your bank supports next-day ACH, then the money would show up the next day, and if your bank supports same-day ACH, you will likely get your money by the end of the day. But in Khaleel's story, he needed the money that second, otherwise, he would have been late to work, which is his primary source of income.

So, how does that actually work? Well, the Push-to-Card transaction works like this:

The end-user inputs a debit card into an app like Venmo or Cash App. Money can be pushed onto that card, simply by selecting that card and pushing to it. This transaction works like a return. So, when you go to your favorite retailer and you return an item that you bought with your debit card, that money is instantly credited to your debit card. The funds are actually available for you to spend immediately.

Visa Direct and Mastercard Send work much in the same way, except that this push transaction doesn't have a related purchase transaction. This is why this Push-to-Card technology is also referred to as an "Original Credit Transaction (OCT)." This is because there wasn't an associated purchase transaction that goes along with this.

WHY SHOULD I WAIT A WEEK TO GET MY PAY?

The technology is fairly new, developed in the last ten years, but only recently has it been getting attention. The technology really gained notoriety when Uber started using it to pay their drivers daily. Uber and Lyft drivers have the option of getting paid via direct deposit by the end of the week, or they can get paid instantly at the end of their shift. They also have the option to cash out multiple times a day. The fee typically ranges between $0.50 to $1.00 per cash out to do this.

Most Lyft drivers in the US use the instant payout functionality. About 80 percent of these drivers have Visa debit cards through their bank, and 20 percent have Mastercard debit cards through their bank. They love the fact that they can get cash whenever they need it. They may not need the money, but the fact that they can access it provides an added level of comfort for these drivers. The technology is fundamentally changing the way we think about getting paid.

PUSH-TO-CARD IS EASY AND FAST

The added benefit of this technology is that it is using the debit card rails provided by Visa or Mastercard. The chances of you having your debit card in your pocket are significantly higher than you having a physical check in your pocket or remembering your account and routing number to your bank off the top of your head. Adding a debit card to an app is as easy as taking a picture of it, as apps use Optical Character Resolution (OCR) to pull in your card numbers. Setting this up in most apps takes less than a minute, and cashing out takes less than fifteen seconds.

Branch uses the Push-to-Card technology to provide its users with a portion of their earned wages early. As a user, they would register for the Branch service by:

1. Adding their debit card.
2. Adding information about where and when they work to their Branch app.
3. Based off of that, Branch can offer its users early access to their earned wages.

4. Move funds immediately to the user's debit card within seconds.

An unexpected car breakdown, an unexpected medical expense, or just gas to get to work, Branch leverages this technology to move money when and where people need it the most at lightning speed.

Branch uses a Merchant Acquirer to facilitate this. The Merchant Acquirer is integrated with Visa Direct and Mastercard Send, so Branch doesn't need to worry about which debit card its users are trying to use.

FOUNDER STORY: RODNEY ROBINSON OF TABAPAY

In 1997, International Business Machines (IBM) coins the term "eBusiness" and doubles down on its service offerings to enable Internet businesses to conduct real transactions on the Internet. One of its earliest customers was PC Flowers, a company founded by William J. Tobin, who linked FTD's 25,000 member florists to the Prodigy network. IBM enabled 485,000 Prodigy subscribers to purchase flowers online for the first time by simply keying in their debit or credit card securely over their dial-up Internet connections, and then getting flowers delivered directly to the doorstep of their loved ones. The man leading this charge at IBM was Rodney Robinson.

Rodney then went on to building IBM's national practice for banking, finance, and securities, where he helped banks offer online bill payment services and built their presence online as the world became more digitized and connected. Here he had to build a depth of experience in payments back when the term "eCommerce" was fairly new and novel. Here he discovered the power of being able to use card-based payments to transact instantly.

After his time at IBM, Rodney went on to product leadership roles at Intuit and a number of tech startups, including Obopay. At Obopay, Rodney and his team were trying to build a Peer-to-Peer technology where people could send money from one flip phone to another flip phone. They inked a deal with Citibank to pilot the program and realized that for this experience to seem instantaneous, they would need to use the card network rails. So, they built a technology that allowed one user to send money from their credit card to another person's credit card. While the concept was interesting, in practice, they learned later on that this technology was more interesting for fast disbursements from businesses. Farmers Insurance then became a customer and used the technology to pay out claims instantly to service providers like auto repair shops, where money could be moved instantly from Farmers Insurance directly to the auto repair shop's credit or debit card. The speed of the transaction was eye-opening, moreover, it was the fact that there was the certainty of delivery, which was offered by the card networks. That is, when the transaction was processed, Farmers was able to get an instant confirmation that the money was delivered. This is something that couldn't be done with traditional ACH.

This experience with Farmers led Rodney to become an entrepreneur and co-found Omney. At Omney, Rodney and his team built the Push-to-Card technology which later went on to become Mastercard Send when it was acquired in 2014. In the early days, Rodney and his team were able to create a transaction that was able to load funds onto a debit or credit card in a manner that looked like an in-store item return, except there wasn't an original purchase transaction for that return to reference. Later on, Visa, Mastercard, Discover, and American Express all created specific transaction types for this type of transaction also referred to as an "Original Credit Transaction (OCT)."

In 2016, Uber announced its Instant Pay offering to all of its drivers, where their 1099 drivers could get paid out daily within seconds using the Push-to-Card technology. This is the moment where this technology really became mainstream, which also coincided with Visa launching their Push-to-Card offering called Visa Direct.

After selling Omney to Mastercard in 2014, Rodney saw the meteoric rise in usage of the Push-to-Card technology amongst 1099 workers like Uber and Lyft Drivers, but he also saw online short-term lenders using the technology to get money into the hands of its users instantly. The only challenge that these short-term lenders had was the ability to collect back from the user using the same debit or credit card. So, Rodney proposed that Mastercard enable both Push and Pull from the same debit or credit card, but the Pull portion meant that Mastercard would need to become a Merchant Acquirer, and, thus, compete against First Data.

Both Visa and Mastercard, being that they are the networks in the middle, need to maintain their stance as the rails moving data and money between Merchant Acquirers and Card

Issuers. Rodney's proposition became politically difficult for Mastercard to do in-house, so Rodney decided to co-found his next startup, Tabapay.

The "Taba" in Tabapay stands for "There and Back Again," and the market that Rodney was trying to build a solution for was for online lenders who were sending money "there" and then eventually needed the funds "back again." To do this, Rodney built an Acquirer Processor from the ground up, integrating with Visa and Mastercard as the primary networks, but also integrating with secondary networks or regional networks such as Pulse, NYCE, Star, and Accel. The idea was to allow users in need of a loan to receive money to their debit or credit card, and then pay it back using the same debit or credit card. In doing this, Tabapay also can serve as an Acquirer Processor for any eCommerce site as well, but with their unique offering of being able to offer both push and pull from a single card, Tabapay has been able to power most of the leading Earned Wage Access providers.

In addition to this technology, Tabapay also has built a proprietary algorithm to help its Merchants get the lowest possible Interchange. It uses its connections with primary and secondary networks to determine which network will yield the lowest Interchange and route the transaction through there. The reality is that 89 percent of the cost to a Merchant, or in this case, a short-term lender, is the cost of Interchange. It is something that can't be negotiated down as it is set by the card networks. The remaining 11 percent is the network assessment that goes directly to the card network, which typically cannot be negotiated down either. Finally, the Acquirer fee can get negotiated down based on transaction volume.

This is the direct cut that is given to a Merchant Acquirer like Tabapay. However, to be able to lower the total cost of the transaction, you need to be smart about how you route the transaction to get the best possible rate as the rates vary from network to network.

An example of this would be if a user was to transact with a Visa Debit card. Tabapay actually has at least three paths where it could route the transaction. The first would be to try running through the Visa's credit network, second would be to run through Visa's debit network (usually Interlink), or run on the card's unaffiliated network (a requirement of the Dodd-Frank Act), which could be something like Pulse, NYCE, or Accel. Depending on which network yields the lowest Interchange, Tabapay will route the transaction through there. In doing so, Tabapay can effectively lower the cost to push or pull funds to the short-term lender through Interchange arbitrage.

As Rodney continued to work with his lending customers, he also realized the need to offer non-card-based options such as ACH. This becomes important in cases where a user takes a loan from the lender on their debit card and then cancels their debit card or "freezes" it. The lender will not be able to pull back the funds because the card is canceled or frozen. Thus, to reclaim funds, the lender needs an alternative that could be pulled back via ACH, which would require the lender to have the account and routing number of the user's checking account. ACH historically would take two to three business days, but now can be done as a same-day ACH if the transaction is invoked before a certain cutoff time during the day. Another more recent technology called Real-Time

Payments (RTP) is a way to send funds instantly, rivaling the speed of Visa Direct and Mastercard Send at a fraction of the cost.

KEY TAKEAWAYS

- Push-to-Card is a fast and reliable way for people to get money sent to their debit cards.
- This technology is changing the way people get paid.
- There is less reliance on having to know your bank account and routing number to receive money.

UP NEXT...

We'll learn how virtual cards can create moments of magic.

CHAPTER 14

PAYMENTS IN ACTION PART 2: VIRTUAL CARDS

HOW CAN VIRTUAL CARDS BE USED TO CREATE MOMENTS OF MAGIC?

In October of 2016, a team of engineers from San Francisco led by Neil Gandhi took a last-minute trip to Las Vegas because they heard about this Hackathon at the Money 2020 conference that could score them $25k if they won. A hackathon is an event held for software developers where the developers come up with an idea (usually a web or mobile app) and have to build it within a short period of time. Hackathons are typically surrounding a theme, and developers can win prizes for their ideas, especially if they use software tools offered by the hackathon sponsors.

Neil and his three other team members booked a room at the Venetian Hotel but realized that they likely wouldn't be sleeping because the hackathon was just for twenty-four hours starting on Saturday afternoon and ending Sunday morning the following day.

They had an idea for a financial advisor that they could speak with using Amazon Alexa. With this, they could get financial advice and also initiate trades, but not knowing too much about payments, the team decided to have conversations with all of the payments and fintech sponsors to see what technologies they could use to bring their idea to life.

They decided to use some APIs from Visa to build out their financial advisor, Warren. They were competing against one hundred teams from around the globe who all converged to Las Vegas to get a shot at winning the $25k prize.[12]

While they were excited about the possibility of winning the $25k prize, they knew that they would probably receive some check in the mail a few weeks later.

This wasn't Visa's plan. Visa partnered with Marqeta and Virtual Incentives to offer the winning team instant access to their earnings via virtual cards that would be issued to each team member at the time of the winning announcement, giving them an opportunity to spend some of their earnings while in Las Vegas and enjoy their moment.

After a grueling twenty-four hours, sleep in their eyes, and nothing more than coffee and Red Bull to fuel them, Neil's team delivered a magical presentation to the judges. It was a huge relief once the presentations were over. Neil and his team took a deep breath in; now it was up to the judges to decide who would be the winners.

---

12   "Visa Developer Champions Win Big at the 2016 Money 20/20 Hackathon," Visa, accessed January 26, 2020.

After what felt like an eternity, the judges walked back into the main hall, and the anticipation built as Visa went through some insights that they saw from the weekend. They then went right into it and announced their two winners. One of which was Neil's team!

Expecting to fill out some long disclosure forms with addresses and such to receive their winnings, Neil's team was pleasantly surprised to find that all they needed to do was provide their driver's license to do a Know Your Customer (KYC) check to ensure that they were eligible to receive a Visa card in the US, and an email address. Minutes later, they received an email from a company called Virtual Incentives[13] congratulating them on winning the Visa Developer Challenge at the Money 2020 Hackathon with their winning amount. Neil's team was four team members including himself, so each team member won a cool $6,250. The email asked the winner if they wanted to get a virtual card right now or wait for a physical card to arrive in the mail in a few days. For those who opted for the virtual card, they were directed to Virtual Incentive's mobile website, which showed their card number. They could use this number to buy things online by keying the card number into their online shopping cart. Alternatively, they could buy things in-store by showing the number to the cashier at the checkout (cashier would key in their card number to process the transaction).

The power of the virtual card was able to grant these team members with instant gratification for their hard work.

---

13 "Virtual Incentives' Technology Delivers Prize Money to Visa Developer Challenge Winners of Money 20/20 Hackathon," PR Newswire, accessed January 26, 2020.

Virtual Incentives had built a gifting platform to create magical experiences just like this, where the reward is instant and gets amplified by being inserted into the moment. Imagine taking a test drive of a car, and before you bring the car back to the dealership, an email is waiting for you with a little thanks from the car company that you can spend anywhere online, or if you really would like a physical card, you can opt for it in the mail. Or why not dynamically generate a reward for an employee who has gone above and beyond for your company, by offering them a reward on the spot with a customized message from you?

Virtual Incentives partnered with Marqeta (an Issuer Processor of cards) to offer this experience by offering both Mastercard and Visa cards. Virtual Incentives is able to customize the email template with the corporation's logo and branding, and if the user opts to receive a physical card in the mail, the Visa card or Mastercard could have the brand's logo at the top of the card, giving more visibility to the brand.

Virtual Incentives offers its customers, typically large Fortune 500 companies, with a web interface to issue cards out to their employees or customers but also provides APIs that can be incorporated into any of their customers' applications. Customers can control the content contained within the email and also upload a corporate image that can be placed on the physical card.

KEY TAKEAWAYS
- Virtual cards can be created quickly and can provide instant gratification to users.

- Virtual cards can be used for online purchases, and in many cases can be added into mobile wallets like Apple Pay or GPay.

UP NEXT...

We'll learn about more proactive ways to manage corporate expenses by killing the expense report.

CHAPTER 15

PAYMENTS IN ACTION PART 3: KILLING THE EXPENSE REPORT

EMPLOYERS AND EMPLOYEES HATE EXPENSE REPORTS; ISN'T THERE A BETTER ALTERNATIVE?

In 2017, there was over $493 billion in small business credit card spent, and it is expected to grow to $686 billion by

2020 according to the Mercator Advisory Group[14]. The industry previously was dominated by American Express, but new modern upstarts are disrupting American Express's stronghold on the industry by providing innovative solutions for small businesses and tech companies. Payments startup Brex raised a total of $281 million as of 2019 with an eye-watering valuation of $2.6 billion.[15] Brex focuses on providing credit cards for young tech companies. More recently, Stripe has announced its own corporate expense card, along with Expensify who, for the past decade, has been focused on making "expense reports suck less." Other notable companies offering modern debit and credit cards include Divvy, Bento for Business, and Emburse.

"We are spending way too much on business meals! We're 40 percent over budget because five new people all of a sudden submitted expense reports, and they didn't know the meal limits we have set!" exclaimed Jessica, corporate controller for a small tech startup in Oakland, California.

Jessica's company is growing very quickly and with that, a lot of new hires, and policies are sometimes ignored or not enforced by the managers. Her company uses an expense management tool like Expensify or Concur. They allow all employees to use their personal credit cards to make purchases and then send the receipts for reimbursement.

14　Brian Riley, "Small Business Credit Cards Have Plenty of Growth Potential in the U.S.," Mercator Advisory Group, accessed on January 26, 2020.

15　Kate Clark, "Brex valued at $2.6N with new cash from Kleiner Perkins," TechCrunch, accessed on January 26, 2020.

One of the major perks of working for an early-stage startup is that you can use your personal credit card and earn points. At larger consulting companies such as Deloitte, you are typically issued a corporate American Express card and you are allowed to keep the points, whereas others, the corporation keeps the points.

The key drawback to using your personal credit card is that if the expense is large and you don't get paid back from your employer in time, you are liable for paying the interest charges. This is what was happening to Emmet, who works for Jessica's company. He was making frequent international trips, and in a month, he could rack up to $15 to $20k in expenses. He would submit these monthly expenses to Jessica via the expense management tool, sometimes a couple of months after the charge was made. Because Jessica was so busy processing all of these expenses, in many cases she wouldn't be able to pay Emmet back until after the credit card's due date. Luckily, Emmet had enough in his bank account to cover this, but if he didn't, he would have incurred late charges on his personal credit card.

How does expense reimbursement work with an expense management tool like Expensify or Concur?

1. Emmet uses his personal card to purchase airline tickets.
2. Because his card is linked to his expense management tool, it shows up automatically in his expense management tool's dashboard.
3. Before the end of the month, Emmet needs to go into the expense management tool and make sure all of the

expense categories are correct on his spend and also add in comments for the expense.

4. He will need to upload receipts for each expense that requires it, typically, anything over $25.
5. Emmet then submits for reimbursement.
6. An email gets sent to Emmet's manager.
7. Emmet's manager opens the expense report and then does a quick review. If something looks strange, he can send it back to Emmet for review.
8. If everything looks reasonable, then he can forward this to Jessica, who will do the final approval.
9. Jessica then gets an email to review Emmet's expenses.
10. She finds that Emmet miscategorized a few of his expenses. She goes in and adjusts them. Sometimes receipts are missing so she needs to email Emmet for the receipts.
11. She then finalizes it, which initiates the payment to Emmet via ACH.
12. Finally, at the end of the month when everyone has submitted their expenses, she will export all the expense records from the expense management tool and then import them into QuickBooks, her accounting software. Most expense management tools also have a direct integration with QuickBooks or other accounting software which feeds in the data automatically.
13. Once Jessica is done closing the books for the month, she then reviews her actual expenses to what was budgeted, here she finds that month after month, the company is overspending on business meals and possibly other expenses.

While this flow is fairly easy to follow, Jessica is only able to know that there is overspending happening until *after* the fact. She's not able to prevent it from happening. She then needs to review all of the expense reports for meals, and then tell the managers which employees are overspending. As it turns out, Emmet was spending over the typical meal limit of $30. However, Emmet does a lot of travel to Tokyo where meals are more expensive.

She has a conversation with Emmet's manager, and he explains that Emmet will need to have a higher meal limit and that's why he approved the expense report. Now, Jessica has to remember that it is okay if Emmet overspends.

These are common challenges that the accounting team and controllers face with expenses. It is never clean and easy, and enforcing corporate standards is tough. This is why a whole new crop of expense management startups like Brex, Emburse, and Divvy have come up to address this by offering their own corporate credit cards, both virtual and physical, along with accounting tools to manage spend more proactively. They realize that small companies don't have the luxury of dealing with overspend on expenses.

Expense rules can be very finite, meaning that each employee could have spend rules applied for each expense, or expense type. So, for example, the default rule for spend at restaurants could be set to $30 per swipe, meaning that if an employee spends more than $30 at a restaurant, then the transaction would get declined.

Another approach is to set a budget per employee for a specific event, so for example, the employee could be allocated $5,000 for a trip. This would include spend on airfare, hotels, meals, and parking. Once the employee exceeds the total budget, the card will start to get declined.

Here is how a typical flow will work with a Divvy expense card program:

1. Emmet receives a card from his employer (typically arrives within a week of signing up, and comes to the corporate HQ unless otherwise specified).
2. Emmet's Manager adds Emmet to his department's budget.
3. Manager allocates a certain amount of this budget to Emmet for his travel expenses.
4. Emmet gets a push notification letting him know that he has been given a budget to spend against.
5. Emmet then goes to IVY restaurant in Tokyo and spends 5500 YEN, which is approximately $55USD.
6. Had he gone over his budget for the trip, the card would have gotten declined, which is real expense control.
7. The waiter then swipes his card, and the transaction is approved.
8. Emmet receives a push notification that the transaction was approved and to close out the expense.
9. Emmet opens up the Divvy mobile app.
10. He ensures that the right expense code of "employee meal" is selected (because the card was swiped at a restaurant, the expense code automatically defaults, but it is always good for Emmet to verify).
11. This restaurant actually provides a receipt through the swipe, so Emmet is shown the receipt in the app. This is done if the restaurant opts into providing this data, commonly referred to as "Track 3 data."

12. If the receipt is not available via Track 3 data, then Emmet is prompted to take a picture of his receipt.
13. Emmet then closes out the expense.
14. He closes out the app.
15. Now the transaction is finalized, he doesn't need to do anything else at the end of the month to submit his expense report.
16. Jessica sees these transactions in real-time.
17. On a weekly basis, she views all of the expense transactions and makes adjustments as needed. Because the push notification happens as soon as the swipe happens, the number of adjustments has gone down for Jessica.
18. With the Divvy QuickBooks integration, all of the expense transactions go into QuickBooks automatically in a "pending" state. Then Jessica can go into QuickBooks and approve these transactions.
19. These transactions are then entered into the QuickBooks accounting ledger.
20. On a weekly basis, Divvy can initiate an ACH Pull transaction, where the week's transactions for Jessica's company is automatically withdrawn from the corporate bank account. She opted into this mode because it makes her life easier and because her company can earn higher points that can later be converted into cash back on a future statement or used for travel rewards through Divvy's travel portal.
21. By paying off the balance on a weekly basis, the credit line of Jessica's company is maintained, which is another added benefit.

REVENUE MODELS FOR EXPENSE MANAGEMENT COMPANIES

Jessica isn't billed anything for offering the Divvy expense platform to her company's employees. Divvy makes its money off of the Interchange earned on all of the credit card spend happening on its platform. This is why Divvy is able to offer its service to enterprises without a Software as a Service (SaaS) fee. In this model, Jessica doesn't have to worry about growing costs as her company grows. Additionally, since there isn't a cost, Jessica can provide an expense card to every employee who might need a card currently or in the future. It is now just part of the onboarding process.

Traditional expense management companies, such as Expensify and Concur, make their money by offering their expense management platform for a monthly Software as a Service fee, so the more employees using the platform at a given employer, the more money is made by these platforms.

KEY TAKEAWAYS

- Debit and credit cards allow for very sophisticated controls to allow for real-time spend.
- Real-time spend controls prevent surprises at the end of the month for finance departments.
- Rich data that comes from the card swipe can be used to complete expense reports on behalf of the user by automatically filling in expense categories and automatically attaching receipts.
- By leveraging Interchange revenue, expense management platforms can be provided for free to the employer and employee.

EVERY COMPANY IS A PAYMENTS COMPANY

———

Now that you have seen how these payments technologies work, it is going to be hard for you to find a company that isn't a Payments Company. Every company won't be providing payments infrastructures like Marqeta, Stripe, Adyen, Tabapay, or Square but rather they will be using payments at its core.

Uber and Lyft both became Payments Companies when they needed the ability to take payments from passengers seamlessly. As they expanded globally, they needed to figure out how to accept payments in all different currencies and different payment methods. Finally, they used card-based payments to build delightful payments experiences for their drivers, all to help them get paid faster. Uber has recently announced a new driver debit card and a consumer credit card and is looking into building even more financial services for its riders and drivers.[16]

Airbnb is also a Payments Company because it needs to be able to accept payments from all over the world and be able to pay out its hosts in multiple different ways. Airbnb has a dedicated group called "Airbnb Payments," which solely focuses on how to make this all work and how best to monetize it (or in many cases, figure out ways to reduce costs of payments). In fact, one of the early experiences that Brian Chesky, Airbnb's CEO, faced when building Airbnb is how awkward it was for a host to ask his guest to pay for the stay. Brian had a situation where he didn't have any cash on him and, thus, it made the experience tense. Although he eventually paid for his stay, he knew that he needed to remove the awkwardness of this experience.

Housecall Pro, a provider of tools for small business owners, or "pros," in the plumbing, landscaping, electrical, and construction space, originally set out as a way for consumers to find local plumbers and electricians and be able to order them on-demand much like an Uber.

It later realized that it had a mission to build tools for these pros so they can run their businesses. This included scheduling tools, invoicing, and accounting tools. One of its major features was to allow consumers to pay their pros via a credit or debit card. This service is now processing millions of

---

16 Andrew J. Hawkins, "Uber Money is the company's latest attempt to expand into financial services," The Verge, accessed on January 26, 2020.

dollars' worth of transactions monthly. In reality, Housecall Pro is also a Payments Company.

By taking the learnings from this book, I hope you can also build a great Payments Company. Every modern business today will need to interact with payments. Now that you know how all of the pieces work, I hope you can come up with some innovative ways to leverage card-based payments, to take your business to the next level.

***

GLOSSARY

___

Term	Description	Reference Chapter
3D Secure	This is a standard for offering cardholders one more layer of security for online transactions. When card numbers are entered into a website to pay for something, 3D Secure will require the cardholder to enter one more form of authentication, such as a one-time-use PIN or passcode, similar to how two-factor authentication works for websites.	4
ACH	ACH or Automated Clearing House is a technology that is offered by the "Clearing House," which is a nonprofit organization. It is a network of banks that have come together to enable the movement of money interbank through the use of bank account and routing numbers.	12

Acquirer Processor	The Merchant Acquirer needs a technology provider that can connect with the payment networks. Usually, the Acquirer Processor will have a piece of hardware in their data centers and a fast network connection directly to the payment networks to request approval of a transaction. Sometimes, the Merchant Acquirer may have built this technology in-house or may rely on a third-party Acquirer Processor to handle this. Examples include Chase Paymentech, Tabapay, and Fiserv.	1
Authorization	Authorization happens at the moment of the swipe, dip, or tap at the payment terminal. This action typically places a hold of funds on the cardholder's account if the cardholder has enough money in their account, or it may decline the transaction if the cardholder doesn't have enough money in their account or if other restrictions on this type of spend apply.	2
Chargeback	When a cardholder doesn't recognize a charge on a credit or debit card, they may request their money back through their Issuing Bank. Chargebacks can also be used in case goods and services have not been provided by the Merchant, but the Merchant refuses to return the money. This step will happen after settlement.	4
Clearing	The term "Clearing" is used primarily by Issuers, but can also be referred to as "Capture" by Merchant Acquirers. Clearing happens toward the end of the day for most Merchants and will factor in tips, transaction reversals, and returns. This is basically the Merchant confirming these transactions are valid and that these funds are ready to be moved or "settled."	3

Co-brand Partner	This is typically a brand or company that is marketing the card. This is the brand shown on the card in addition to the card network brand. In some cases, this brand will appear on the front of the card without the Issuing Bank, and in other cases, it may appear on the front with the Issuing Bank.	8
Direct Deposit	A direct deposit is a type of ACH transfer that typically comes from an employer into an employee's bank account.	12
EMV Chip Card	EMV originally stood for "Europay, Mastercard, Visa," who established the technical standard for encoding the card data onto a secure chip placed on a card. Cards with this type of chip and data encryption can be "dipped" into card terminals to pay for goods and services in a secure way. This method of storing card data is considered far more secure than data stored on the magnetic stripe on the back of a card used to "swipe." The EMV standard is now managed by EMVco, which is now a consortium of financial companies.	4
Independent Sales Organization (ISO)	An ISO is granted a license to sell Merchant acquiring services from a Merchant Acquirer such as Wells Fargo or Chase Paymentech.	7
Interchange	Interchange is a fee that is sent from the Merchant to the Issuing Bank of the card being swiped. This fee is predetermined by the card networks based on a number of factors.	11
Issuer	An Issuer or Issuing Bank's function is to underwrite the user by giving them a bank account, a debit card, and potentially access to credit facilities and a credit card. Examples include Citibank, Wells Fargo, US Bank, and Chase.	1

Issuer Processor	The Issuer needs a technology provider that can connect with the payment networks. Usually, the Issuer Processor will have a piece of hardware in their data centers and a fast network connection directly to the payment networks to approve or decline a transaction. Sometimes, the Issuer may have built this technology in-house or may rely on a third-party Issuer Processor to handle this. Examples include Marqeta, Tsys, Galileo, and i2c.	1
Know Your Customer (KYC)	KYC or Know Your Customer is a practice in the banking and finance industry used to attach some form of identity to the user of a product.	9
Merchant Acquirer	The Merchant Acquirer goes out and acquires Merchants and provides them the tools and facilities to accept and process card-based payments. Examples include Citibank, Wells Fargo, US Bank, and Chase.	1
Payments Facilitator (PF or Pay-Fac)	This is a layer on top of a Merchant Acquirer. Payments Facilitators can typically onboard Merchants very quickly, and offer out-of-the-box hardware and software to enable a Merchant to start accepting card-based payments quickly.	7
Payment Network	Sometimes referred to as a "Card Scheme" or just as a "Network." Examples of Payment Networks include Visa, Mastercard, American Express, and Discover. These Payment Networks provide the rails for card-based transactions to occur. They sit in between Acquirers and Issuers and pass messages back and forth to make the transaction happen. The Payment Networks also set the communications rules and standards that the Acquirers and Issuers need to adhere to.	1

Payment Service Provider (PSP)	A PSP is an aggregator of payment methods. It allows a website operator to get paid via debit cards, mobile wallets, and financing schemes.	7
Program Manager	The program manager is the one who is managing the day-to-day operations of the card program including settlement, fraud management, and maintaining the relationship with the Issuing Bank, card manufacturer, card network, and the cardholder.	8
Real-Time Payments (RTP)	RTP is a way to push money within seconds by sending money directly to a bank account offered by The Clearing House.	12
Settlement	Settlement is the actual movement of money from the cardholder's bank account, the Issuing Bank, to the Merchant's bank account, the Acquiring Bank. This movement of money typically happens via Fedwire as instructed by the payment networks.	3
Wire Transfer	Wire transfer is a way to move money (usually large dollar amounts) from one bank to another securely and quickly by using the account and routing numbers of the sending and receiving banks.	12

***

ACKNOWLEDGMENTS

———

Writing and publishing a book has been a lifelong dream of mine, and I really couldn't have made this happen without my family and friends. To my loving wife, Mona, who has always been by my side and the only person in this universe that truly understands me. To my three amazing children, Misha, Mikal, and Marina, who have kept me on my toes and given me the daily inspiration to keep moving forward. To my father and hero, Mustafa, who has pushed me to be my best. To my loving mother, Wajahat, who taught me to be a good and humble person.

There have also been some amazing folks who took the time to add content to this book by providing their knowledge and mentorship:

- Jason Gardner, CEO, Marqeta
- Zach Perrett, CEO, Plaid
- Rodney Robinson, CEO, Tabapay
- David Galvan, VP, Business Development and Strategic Alliances, Mastercard
- Rick Song, CEO, Persona

- Atif Siddiqi, CEO, Branch
- Ricardo Navarro, Director of Community, Visa

Through the book writing process, I had a number of friends and family who really supported me by being early readers of the book, providing edits and suggestions. These folks also contributed financially by buying early copies of the book and helping me through the publishing journey:

Aayush Upadhyay
Aayush, we met when you were a senior in college and I am so proud of everything you have accomplished. Thank you for your support throughout the years!

Abhay Puskoor
Abhay, thank you for your support and your passion for looking into companies that are under the radar. I learned from you that many companies at the outset are incredibly boring, but when you go a layer deeper, they are very interesting. I hope one day to learn more from you on this and help uncover these hidden gems.

Adam Patton
Adam, you probably are the best designer I've ever worked with and thank you for always taking on initiatives with a smile. Thank you for challenging me and always looking to making the experience better for our customers.

Adrianne Ho
Adrianne, you are the best PR professional I've ever met. I wanted to thank you for all of the help you provided in the

production of this book and also, in general, helping me bring back my love of PR and marketing.

Alex Gillette
Alex, thanks for being persistent. Your guidance during the writing of this book was paramount to making the chapters really shine. Thank you for all of the time you put into helping make this book great!

Alex Hegevall Clarke
Alex, thank you for your amazing partnership over the last year. You really have a knack for understanding our business needs and how your product can best optimize for that. We couldn't build our business without your help. Thank you for being an amazing listener and helping us overcome some of our biggest challenges.

Alex Heinen
Alex, it is so rare to find an engineer who understands products as well as you. Thank you for always being willing to listen to ideas and then coming up with plans on how to execute them. Most importantly, thank you for your friendship.

Ali Siddiqui
Ali, my cousin, and my inspiration for writing. When you started your sports blogging, I decided I should get back into blogging too. Thank you for always being there for me.

Arthur Zhao
Arthur, my dream finance guy... Thank you for being an amazing partner. You taught me so much about finance. While it was aggravating when we were in it, I look back on

the days where we spent days just pouring through invoice after invoice trying to understand how the networks bill for their services. Thank you for your support and friendship.

Asim Siddiqui

Asim, my fellow IBMer. Thanks for being such a great friend and always making your house available for impromptu breakfasts. Your fridge is impressively stocked!

Brady Burkett

Thank you, Brady, for your support! Really looking forward to working with you as we think about transacting internationally.

Brian Miller

Brian, my MIS buddy. After almost twenty years, I randomly bump into you at Chipotle. I'm so glad that we were able to reconnect. Thank you for your positive energy. Looking forward to bringing more Fintech to Minneapolis with you!

Chris Jackson

Chris, my dear friend. Thank you for always keeping me in line and on track. You are the best project manager I've ever met. I can always count on you to get things done. Thank you so much for your support!

Christie Kim

Christie, thank you for being an amazing partner. From our random encounter a year back, you taught me that there are better ways to identify good users. Thank you for changing my perspective on KYC. I'm really excited about our partnership and thank you for your continued support.

Chris Chin

EDF, Cross Border, FX, and the never-ending fees project, thanks, Chris, for being thorough and working with me to build a great design. I really enjoyed working with you at Marqeta and thank you for the continued support throughout the years.

Damon Allison

Damon, who would have thought that almost twenty years after college that we would be working together! Thank you for leveling up the team, I'm so excited about the stuff we will be working on. Thank you for your support!

Dan Osburn

Dan, one of the main reasons the Marqeta platform is so great. You taught me to always think through the details and I am so glad that we were able to partner to build such an amazing product. Thank you for joining me on the journey learning about payments, and for your continued support!

Dave Matter

Dave, you are the reason I got into payments in the first place and I will forever be grateful to you. Thank you for your wisdom, guidance, and inspiration over the years. Thank you for taking a chance on an old high school friend.

Dave White

Dave, the man who taught me about Agile and Jira. An amazing product manager and partner. We really had some amazing times together building Marqeta, I still remember your inspiring talks with the developers, talking about the true potential of what we were building. Thank you for your inspiration and wisdom through the years!

Dave Camburn

Dave, thank you for sourcing and always finding great people to work with. You have introduced me to so many amazing people, and thank you so much for supporting this book!

Dave Tran

Dave, my dream product manager… Thank you for being an amazing partner, helping move a scheduling company into a Payments Company. You really helped make my job easier, and I look forward to all the great things we are going to build together. I appreciate your support in getting this book into the market!

Dhiren Patel

Dhiren, my favorite "lunch buddy" and roommate. You have always been there to listen and bounce off crazy business ideas. Thank you for making our first venture, Go Mongo, a reality. Thank you for your continued support throughout the years!

Edith Mendiola

Edith, my dear, you taught me everything about settlement and how the networks operate. It was you who was able to find all of the bugs in the system. Any time I am reconciling, I channel my "inner Edith" and make sure that the numbers always tie out. Thank you for always being an amazing mentor and always bringing a smile to my face.

Eli Malone-Shkurkin

Eli, you make data beautiful. I hope this book can live up to your expectations. Thank you for your support and inspiration!

Eric Bachman

Eric, thank you for being such an amazing mentor. I learned so much from you about payments and I owe a lot of knowledge and content in this book to you.

Eric Koester

Eric, you are my #1 supporter! Thank you for opening up your book writing course to me. The process has been eye-opening and you have always been there to push me through it. Publishing a book has been a lifelong dream of mine and you were able to make it happen.

Errol Pinto

Errol, the hardest working man in the world. You are a true inspiration and one of the main drivers that kept me going. Thank you for always being there for me, especially in the toughest times, and especially when I was in Dubai.

Fahad Siddiqui

Fahad, thank you for being my best friend. We fought a lot but at the end of it, I'm so fortunate to have a brother like you. Thank you for your continued support. I am so happy to be back in Minnesota with you!

Fareesa Dastagir

Fareesa, my kid sister, thank you for always sticking with me. Thank you for always helping me turn my crazy ideas into reality. From running social media campaigns for an orange blobby character to helping me promote this book, you have always been amazing.

Gentry Davies

Gentry, really excited to have a product manager like you in my professional circle. I'm really excited about all the things you are doing, and thank you for your willingness to help make this book the best book out there in the payments space.

Hasnain Zaidi

Hasnain, while I was writing business plans about making a version of Chipotle, but with Indian food, you actually were out there doing it. Thank you for being such an inspiration and friend.

Jajeev Nithiananda

Jajeev, I will never be able to compete with your amazing Ninja Turtle drawing abilities. Thank you for always supporting me, from the days of building Go Mongo to now, you have always been a positive influence on me. You also pushed me to be a better product manager.

John Beadle

John, my right-hand man. You are the only guy that thinks on the exact same wavelength as me. I literally can think something and you already know what needs to be done. Thank you for always being with me, from hauling one hundred pizzas with me to helping build out Startup Weekend in the Bay Area, you are a true friend. Thank you for being there for me always.

John Tullis

John, it is rare to find someone who knows so much about payments and yet so humble. I learned a lot from you and thank you for always being there when I needed help.

Joshua Schaub

Josh, you certainly know how to keep me out of trouble. I really appreciate your perspective on startup law. It is rare to find an attorney that looks at the needs of the business first before getting into the nitty-gritty of the specific laws.

Kamaljit Vilkhoo

Kamaljit, thank you for your continued support throughout the years. You took me under your wing and taught me all about data modeling, which ultimately got me to where I am today.

Kausi Ahmed

Kausi, my friend and confidant. You are always there for me. Every time I got on the Bart, I hoped that I would run into you so we can spend thirty minutes getting to work talking about business, life, kids, or just about anything. Thank you for being such a great listener and supporter.

Keenan Simmons

Keenan, one of the brightest product managers I've ever met. I am so happy to have the opportunity to work with you and am so proud of everything you have accomplished. Thank you for your wisdom and willingness to listen.

Keith Armstrong

Keith, you crashed at my house in San Francisco then we ran the largest Startup Weekend event ever, MEGA! Thanks for always being there to listen and bounce around ideas over the years.

Ken Pascal

Ken, you have always been an amazing supporter from the first Startup Weekend events we ran together, to General Assembly, and now to this book. It is hard to find someone as thoughtful and supportive as you.

Kevin Young

Kevin, young and hungry. I could always count on you to give me the insight into what customers are really looking for. Thank you for your friendship and support!

Khalid Ali

Khalid, after seeing all of the work you put into your book, I was inspired to write as well. Thank you for always being there and providing your guidance.

Hira Khan

Hira, you truly are amazing and an inspiration on how to be strong when faced with adversity. When I think of examples of people who I would like to be like, it would be you. I can only wish I had your strength. Thank you for always being selfless and providing your loving support.

Kristine Borghino

Kristine, so many of the things I learned about finance and accounting came from you. You are the inspiration to one of my chapters. I value our time together from even back in the Emeryville days where we sat and tried to figure out how to get those bills out to our customers. Thank you for your support and inspiration!

Kyle Nowakowski
Thank you, Kyle, for your support!

Louise Murphy
Louise, you taught me the value of being persistent. You are probably one of the best sales leaders I've ever met, and I love how you were able to craft a solution that so closely matched what we needed. Thank you for being an amazing friend throughout the years!

Luke Tuttle
Luke, I was pretty bummed out that we couldn't work together, but I wanted to say that I admire everything you have built at Klarna. Thank you so much for your support and for lending me your expertise in payments for this book.

Mehmet Ekin Uygur
Mehmet (Ekin), thank you for always being the smiling face in the office. You somehow always make my day better. Looking forward to building something really big with you, and thank you for always being willing to change and adapt to move the business forward. Thank you for your support!

Melissa Keir
Melissa, from back in the Emeryville days, you have always been an amazing friend, always willing to listen. I am so glad that we were able to learn about payments together,

deciphering the cryptic reports from Visa and Mastercard to helping explain to our banking partners how to "move money." Thanks for your support for my book, I hope it meets your expectations!

Mike Adorno
Mike, the adventures we've been on! From the time we thought we were being attacked by the Yakuza to the good times at Babson. Thank you for always being willing to meet up with me! I really appreciate all of the support!

Mike Borel
Mike, my fellow IBMer, it was always great working with you and in general discussing life. Thanks for the support over the years!

Michael Gonzalez
Michael, thanks once again for your friendship, and for helping me bring this book to publication!

Mona Khan
To the love of my life, Mona. Everything that I have accomplished is due to you. Thank you for always being by my side and supporting me. Because of your willingness to take a wild journey to Dubai, I was able to learn about Payments, which is the inspiration for this book. Thanks for always making the big gambles with me, and looking forward to a lifetime of adventures with you! I love you.

Morgan Reed
Morgan, thanks for introducing me to what actually happens on Capitol Hill. You gave me an opportunity to testify in

front of Congress which has been one of my life goals. Thank you for your continued support and guidance.

Mudassir Azeemi
Mudassir, always there to listen to crazy ideas and provide practical feedback. I am honored to have someone as bright as you as a friend.

Murtuza "Chachaba" Siddiqui
Chachaba, who has been there for me since the day I was born. You raised me and always guided me to the right path in life, for which I am eternally grateful. Every time I felt I was falling, I knew that Chachaba would be there to catch me.

Mustafa "Puppa" Siddiqui
Puppa, my true hero. It was you who always pushed me to be my best. Thank you for being the example of how to be a great human being. I hope the book lives up to your expectations.

Nicholas Straight
Nicholas, you are an incredibly talented artist and I am so humbled that you agreed to work on the illustrations for this book with me. You really made this book shine.

Nili Waypa
Nili, I am so excited about all of the things you have accomplished since graduating. Your continued enthusiasm for startups and the Minnesota Tech Scene is an inspiration.

Nitin Arneja
Nitin, I will always bench press more than you. Thank you for being my best friend in college. In many ways, you

helped shape my career and you even convinced me to move to California, which was probably the best thing that could have happened to me. Thank you for laying down the path for me, I am forever grateful for your guidance and friendship.

Noreen Mohiuddin
Noreen Apa, thank you and Amer Bhai for always supporting me in my crazy endeavors.

Patricia McPeak
Patricia, you taught me so much about being the customer's advocate. So many of the things that you taught me still stay with me.

Patrick Delaney
Patrick, thank you for your friendship through the years, you have been a true inspiration, always looking for ways to do good in the world.

Paul Raythattha
From back in the early days of building an edTech startup, Paul, you were a huge supporter and peer. I really value your friendship and willingness to share war stories. Thank you for your continued support!

Pranav Kariwala
Pranav, thank you for your friendship over the years. It is always amazing to see how the large payments providers are innovating. I appreciate the support for the book!

Prerak Trivedi

Prerak, I really enjoyed our time working together at Marqeta. It is rare to find someone with your engineering skills that understands the business of payments.

Puneet Bysani

Puneet, you are probably one of the best data architects I've ever met and have always enjoyed you challenging me to be better. Thank you for your friendship and support!

Ray Hill

Ray, one of my closest friends at Marqeta. Thank you for always keeping me grounded. It was always nice looking past my monitor and seeing your smiling face!

Rebecca Kersey

Rebecca, it is rare to find a payments professional with the kind of experience that you have. Thank you for being a sounding board and helping me promote this book. You are awesome and can't wait to see what you do next!

Rohan Suryadevara

Rohan, thank you for always being open to getting a Dosa with me. I have always enjoyed our conversations and appreciate your approach to solving problems. Thank you for your support always!

Safura "Sureya Auntie" Hussain

Sureya Auntie, thank you for always being there and being my Boston Mom. I cherish the time we were able to spend together while I was going to Babson.

Salman Ansari

It's really tough to think about going to Jummah without you, Salman. One of my earliest friends when I moved to San Francisco, you have always been there for me. As we both got married, it is so amazing that our wives are such close friends now too. I really miss being near you, but I am so glad to know that I can always count on you for support and guidance.

Salman Syed

Salman, I learned so much about the value of creating win-win solutions from you. You are a tremendous sales leader and a tremendous partner. Thank you for your continued support!

Sam Rosen

From co-founding the Entrepreneurship club with me back when we were in school to helping me get reconnected with the Minnesota business community now, you have always been an amazing friend and mentor. Thank you for your continued support!

Sandy Lo

Sandy, the voice of reason. It was so much fun working with you to build out our financial systems and try to bring some automation at a time when the company was growing like crazy. Thank you for your friendship and support!

Sarah Aleem

Sarah, one of my oldest friends in the Bay Area. Thank you for your continued friendship and enthusiasm for startups. From supporting me when launching Go Mongo, to now, I always know I can lean on you for support. Thank you so much for taking the time to review the contents of this book to make sure it is all good from a legal perspective.

Sasha DeMarre
Sasha, not only did you help me get this book to publication, but you bought it with a card we built together! You have been an unbelievable partner in getting our solutions out to market. Thank you for your drive and passion. Thank you for your support and friendship!

Saul Shum
Saul, thanks for always being there. From being my milk drinking buddy during pub crawls, to always providing your wisdom while at Babson.

Sean Clark
Sean, thank you for being such an amazing partner. You helped a fledgling startup navigate through the massive ship called Mastercard. Thanks for taking a chance on me, and providing this amazing support for the past year.

Sheraz Malik
Sheraz bhai, you have always inspired me to be my best. From all of the events we ran at the University of Minnesota to evaluating different business ideas, you have always been someone I can rely on. Thank you for your support!

Sikander Syed
Sikander, you have been an inspiration, proving that when you put your heart into something, you can win. While this

isn't roller hockey, I hope to follow your example. Thank you for your support!

Song Chin
Song, my coffee buddy and confidant. Thank you for always listening, advising, and constantly pushing me to think about the customer. I learned so much from you about payments but more importantly about leadership. Thank you for being part of the book and your support!

Sudheer Sadhu
My dear friend Sudheer, one of the earliest believers. We have been through so much together, and I am so proud of what we have built. Thank you for your support and friendship.

Sumera Islam
Sumera Apa, my oldest cousin in Minnesota. Thank you for your guidance, wisdom, and continuous support. You have always been so easy to chat with and someone who I can always turn to for an unbiased, genuine opinion. Thank you for your support!

Sushir Amarnath
My good friend Sushir. We went through a lot together and I'm so proud of what you have accomplished. Always be your best, be humble, and you will win. Thanks for the continued support.

Todd Schmalenberger
Todd, thanks for giving a twenty-five-year-old developer a shot at leading a development team while in Japan. I learned so much from you about leadership and delivering a great

project. I am so grateful for all of the support you have given through the years.

Tony Grotte
Tony, my oldest friend. From the Chuck E. Cheese Birthday parties in kindergarten through high school graduation, it has been so amazing knowing you. Really happy that we were able to reconnect after such a long time and share our love for software development. Thanks for all the support!

Vasundhara Chetluru
Vasundhara, thank you for connecting with me and sharing with me the innovative company you are building. I hope you build the next fintech unicorn!

Vishakha Gupta
Vishakha, you are a force to be reckoned with. I admire your drive and passion for everything you do. I am so excited about your new role and your progression in product management. I know you are going to do some big things!

Vishal Arya
Vishal, I very much enjoyed our talks together while we were both at Marqeta. Thank you so much for your support of the book!

Wajahat "Mumma" Siddiqui
To the woman who raised me, I owe everything to you. You were the one who instilled in me all of my values and taught me to be a good human being. Your love has inspired me to always keep doing my best.

Wasib Muhammad
Wasib, thank you for asking me the deep questions about payments. Our conversations helped frame out many of the topics in this book. I really appreciate your friendship and support!

Zach McGillis
Zach, I never knew that a random encounter with a jock in a computer lab could have sparked a friendship like ours. Thank you for always being so supportive over the years.

Zach Boerger
Zach, from the good times back in the Bay Area where we ran Startup Weekend events to now working together in building the next big startup. You showed me how important it was to stay connected with people.

Zaki Khan
Zaki, we grew up together and you are one of my oldest friends. When I was trying to learn about the Minneapolis tech scene, you graciously introduced me to your old boss, who ultimately got me to my current startup. I am so thankful for your friendship and continued support! Thank you for helping me get back to Minnesota!

Finally, I wanted to thank the team at New Degree Press including Eric Koester, Brian Bies, Stephanie McKibben, Cass Lauer, and Amanda Brown for helping me get this thing published.

***

APPENDIX

———

INTRODUCTION

Cornfield, Jill. "Bankrate survey: Just 4 in 10 Americans have savings they'd rely on in an emergency." Bankrate. Accessed on January 26, 2020.

https://www.bankrate.com/finance/consumer-index/money-pulse-0117.aspx

"Payment Cards in Circulation Worldwide - Projected." Nilson Research. October 2019, Issue 1162. Accessed on January 26, 2020.

https://nilsonreport.com/publication_chart_and_graphs_archive.php?1=1&year=2019

Harris, Matthew. "Fintech: The Fourth Platform - Part One." Forbes. Accessed on January 26, 2020.

https://www.forbes.com/sites/matthewharris/2019/11/19/fintech-the-fourth-platform-part-one/#a943efecb28c

CHAPTER 2

"The Federal Reserve Payments Study - 2018 Annual Supplement." Federal Reserve. Accessed on January 26, 2020.

https://www.federalreserve.gov/paymentsystems/2018-December-The-Federal-Reserve-Payments-Study.htm

CHAPTER 4

"Lost or Stolen Credit, ATM, and Debit Cards." Federal Trade Commission: Consumer Information. Accessed on January 26, 2020.

https://www.consumer.ftc.gov/articles/0213-lost-or-stolen-credit-atm-and-debit-cards

"Chargeback Stats." Chargebacks 911. Accessed on January 26, 2020.

https://chargebacks911.com/chargeback-stats/

CHAPTER 5

"Payment Cards in Circulation Worldwide - Projected." Nilson Research. October 2019, Issue 1162. Accessed on January 26, 2020.

https://nilsonreport.com/publication_chart_and_graphs_archive.php?1=1&year=2019

CHAPTER 6

"Marqeta Consumer Behavior Survey." Marqeta. February 2019. Accessed on January 26, 2020.

https://marqeta.cdn.prismic.io/marqeta%2Fc52f2f4f-7c99-4659-8aa2-c0a75695d977_marqeta+consumer+behavior+survey+download.pdf

Son, Hugh. "This branchless bank quadrupled its customer base to 4 million in a single year." CNBC. Accessed on January 26, 2020.

https://www.cnbc.com/2019/06/12/chime-has-quadrupled-its-customer-base-to-4-million-in-a-single-year.html

CHAPTER 10

"TD Bank's Annual Consumer Spending Index Reveals Credit Knowledge Gap Exists Among Millenials." PR Newswire. Accessed on January 26, 2020.

https://www.prnewswire.com/news-releases/td-banks-annual-consumer-spending-index-reveals-credit-knowledge-gap-exists-among-millennials-300810766.html

CHAPTER 12

"A modern guide to ACH: Everything you need to know to start accepting ACH payments." Plaid. Accessed on January 26, 2020.

https://go.plaid.com/rs/495-WRE-561/images/Plaid-Modern-guide-to-ACH.pdf

CHAPTER 14

"Visa Developer Champions Win Big at the 2016 Money 20/20 Hackathon." Visa. Accessed January 26, 2020. https://usa.visa.com/visa-everywhere/innovation/money2020-hackathon.html

"Virtual Incentives' Technology Delivers Prize Money to Visa Developer Challenge Winners of Money 20/20 Hackathon." PR Newswire. Accessed January 26, 2020.

https://www.prnewswire.com/news-releases/virtual-incentives-technology-delivers-prize-money-to-visa-developer-challenge-winners-of-money2020-hackathon-300371335.html

CHAPTER 15

Riley, Brian. "Small Business Credit Cards Have Plenty of Growth Potential in the U.S." Mercator Advisory Group. Accessed on January 26, 2020.

https://www.mercatoradvisorygroup.com/Templates/BlogPost.aspx?id=6866&blogid=25506

Clark, Kate. "Brex valued at $2.6N with new cash from Kleiner Perkins." TechCrunch. Accessed on January 26, 2020. https://techcrunch.com/2019/06/11/brex-series-c2/

CONCLUSION

Hawkins, Andrew J. "Uber Money is the company's latest attempt to expand into financial services." The Verge. Accessed on January 26, 2020.

https://www.theverge.com/2019/10/28/20936727/uber-money-fintech-debit-credit-cards-finance-digital-wallets